ISLAMIC RIVALRY

ISIS And IRAN
Are Fighting For The Heart Of Islamic Identity

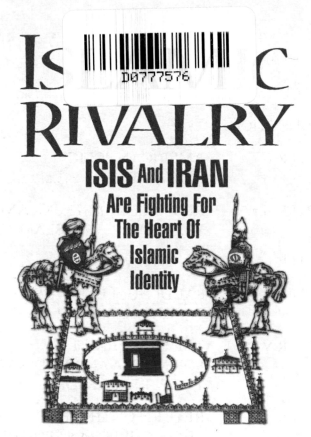

Direct inquires to:
Dennis Avi Lipkin aka/Victor Mordechai
P.O. Box 18209, Jerusalem, Israel 91181
Website: www.vicmord.com
Email: *vicmord2001@yahoo.com*

1st Printing - 5,000 copies
June 2015

TABLE OF CONTENTS

ISLAMIC RIVALRY
ISIS AND IRAN ARE FIGHTING FOR THE HEART OF ISLAMIC IDENTITY

PREFACE

Before getting into the subjects of this book, I feel I must first offer some words of praise firstly to my God, the God of Abraham, Isaac and Jacob for His unbounded blessings and mercies endowed on me for the first 66 years of my life and until this moment. The blessing uttered under these circumstances is:

ברוך אתה השם אלוקינו מלך
העולם שהחיינו , וקיימנו והגיענו לזמן הזה.

Blessed art thou, O Lord our God, King of the Universe, who has given us life, sustained us and brought us to this time.

I suppose any person can, at age 66, relate one's entire lifetime experiences with many complaints and frustrations, but my purpose here is to focus on just how close to death I was as my heart was slowing down, perilously, to 30 beats a minute as a result of a brutal lifestyle of spending on the average six months of the year driving and flying and driving around the world to deliver my message. I wasn't able to eat right or exercise and lived the life of the extreme: of meeting timetables, and pressure to produce a new book every few years as well as CD's and DVD's and also do radio and TV messages in addition to appearing in churches, synagogues, and political-civic meetings. – There was too much tension living out of suitcases and not being in my home in Israel.

My wife and primary care doctor monitored this two year downturn in my heart's function until finally it was decided I needed a pacemaker (June 2013) and a few months later a stent (January 2014). My wife, Rachel, insisted on the best surgeons in Israel to perform these operations and as a result, I have been given a new lease on life. It is as if I became twenty years younger and am now able to continue serving God, which is what I have been continuing to do after 26 years on the road, and like Moses, hope to continue to do until 120 years of age.

It also makes me appreciate how tenuous our lives are, how temporary, and how short-lived. For those of us who believe in God, we can all be taken at any time, and so every moment is precious. There is a saying: "God's gift to us is our life. Our gift to God is what we do with our lives."

So, therefore, all my attentions are to serving God, who chooses whom He will to serve Him. Our actions will be judged in eternity and are aimed at preparing the world to do that which God expects from us to do which is to be a blessing to all nations, to bless this Earth and to tend His garden.

I also wanted to bless the memory of my parents and brother who are no longer among the living. My father and brother died this last year in 2014, leaving me and my sister as survivors. It has not been an easy year! I also wanted to praise my sister, who is a Proverbs 31 woman and who took care of both my parents and brother in their sicknesses while I was far away either in Israel or on the road doing my work and was unavailable to help, much to my sadness and regret. May God give my sister a long life for honoring her mother and father, as it says in the Bible.

And, of course, much praise must go to my wife, Rachel, my two sons, Aaron and Jacob, my daughters-in-law, and of course my nine wonderful grandchildren that God has blessed me with.

As it says in Psalm 128:

"Praiseworthy is each person who fears the Lord, who walks in His paths. When you eat the labor of your hands, you are praiseworthy, and it is well with you. Your wife shall be like a fruitful vine in the inner chambers of your home; your children shall be like olive shoots surrounding your table. Behold! For so is blessed the man who fears God. May God bless you from Zion, and may you gaze upon the goodness of Jerusalem, all the days of your life. And may you see children born to your children, peace upon Israel."

Though it is not the subject of this book, the registration process of the Bible Bloc Party here in Israel is continuing, slowly but surely until we reach the final goal of 100 signatures which I hope to achieve in the coming weeks before the printing of this book in June, 2015. At that time, I am planning to reprint "Israel's Bible Bloc", my fourth book, upon the birth of the Israel Bible Bloc/Gush Hatanakhi Party. So I must thank God for allowing me to complete this mission and enter the history books as the founder for the first time in two thousand years of a Judeo-Christian alliance and Western Civilization party in Israel's Knesset as well. Now, all I have to do is to stay alive, keep healthy from now on, and get elected to the Knesset in the next elections, officially scheduled for 2019, though as often happens could take place much sooner as they usually do due to the vicissitudes of Israeli politics.

Finally, I wanted to thank God again for allowing me to live in these most unbelievable times. We are all witnesses to God's unending miracles: that the Jewish People has survived for over 4,000 years. The Jewish State of Israel was resurrected in 1948 and has been reaching new heights of achievement in so many areas. God's word in His Bible is being verified every day, especially with the home-coming of millions of Jews from all over the world to the Jewish homeland in Israel.

We are the generation that is witnessing more fulfillment of God's word and His prophecies than any other generation in the last 2,000 years. God is allowing all those who wish to, to participate in this same fulfillment of His prophecies.

It is to that purpose that I write this my seventh book, and dedicate it to God, to Israel, to my family, and to the entire human race.

Finally, may God continue to bless my wife, Rachel, my two sons, Aaron and Jacob, my daughters-in-law, and my nine grandchildren. I believe God takes care of me and my family if I take care of His mission.

INTRODUCTION

Every time I write a book, I think: "That's it! No more books." It is not easy to write a book. One must put aside one's family and private life and earthly enjoyments to sit behind a computer for months at a time of dedication to the project. Then one must find a publisher, and if there is no publisher, one must self-publish. This indeed was the case in the publication of my first six books.

In my case, being considered a radical author, I ended up having to self-publish my books, which involves a financial commitment, and mostly, the commitment to leave home in Israel, travel worldwide, lecture in churches, synagogues, and civic groups; actively participate in radio and TV shows, and now form a Judeo-Christian Western Civilization and Democracy Bible Bloc Party in Israel, run for office and prepare for the massive homecoming to Israel of millions of Jews and in many cases their non-Jewish spouses and progeny. The last subject is covered in my fourth book: "Israel's Bible Bloc," which I am planning to reprint in a second edition as the Bible Bloc Party is about ready to be registered.

This, my seventh book: *"Islamic Rivalry"* follows six previous books which dealt with evidence that Islam was a global threat. It included various articles from the press, military intelligence type information I had acquired both in the Israel Defense Forces as well as the Prime Minister's office, results of private investigation activities I was conducting along the Canadian and Mexican borders with the US as well as in Europe, and finally, quoting from the Bible and the Islamic sources to show that the Islamic threat was a Satanic religious threat to the entire human race. This first book grew in five editions from 63 pages in the first edition in 1995 to 286 pages in the fifth and final edition in 1997.

My second book, *"Christian Revival for Israel's Survival"* was a follow-up to my first book and included new updated information but emphasized the significance of political and economic non-Muslim allies and alliances of the Islamic anti-Semitic, anti-Christian and anti-biblical forces.

My third book: *"Islamic Threat Updates Almanac #1 – 5763"* was written in 2003, a year after the 9/11 attacks in the US. It included updated articles and information I gathered during the twelve months following the 9/11 disaster showing that the Moslems were now even more emboldened to attack the West after the relative ease with which they succeeded on 9/11.

My fourth book: *"Israel's Bible Bloc"* (2006) was the summation of what I considered already in 1998 to be the answer to this Islamic threat, a Judeo-Christian alliance globally as well as in Israel to save Israel and the world from Islam. My faith tells me that either the Jews and Christians "hang together" or we will hang on the gallows, be shot in the head or be beheaded, separately. This is the reason for the creation of this new political party in the Israeli political system that will bring about this alliance which defends not only Israel and the Jewish People, but also the Christians who believe in the same God of Abraham, Isaac, and Jacob, the same Old Testament and of course agree that the Messiah is a Jew from Israel who speaks Hebrew. Finally, all of humanity can subscribe to this ideology to defend the human race from the threat of satanic annihilation by Islam.

My fifth book: *"Islam Prophesied in Genesis"* (2010) deals with the ultimate struggle between Islam and the civilized world. In my opinion an in depth study of the Book of Genesis shows the diametrically opposed contentiousness of Islam with Judaism and Christianity. The Book of Genesis explains how the Creation was destroyed by the Flood because of the evil of the human race. God then "re-did" the creation with Noah and his family. My book also contrasted God with Satan, good with evil, peace versus war, love versus hate, Ishmael versus Isaac, Esau versus Jacob as well as all the other challenges facing Abraham, Isaac and Jacob as they founded a dynasty that was to become a nation in Egypt.

My sixth book: *"Return to Mecca"* continued with this natural growth of the Children of Israel from a family to a nation during the period of slavery in Egypt as illustrated in the Book of Exodus, the remaining three books of the Torah and then in some of the other books of the Tanakh (Old Testament).

We see, I believe, another answer to the Islamic Threat. This book basically tries to identify the borders of Israel as promised by God in Deuteronomy 11 that Israel's borders are from Lebanon in the North to the Arabian Peninsula in the South, the Great Sea (Mediterranean) to the West and the Euphrates to the East. The emphasis in this book is to define the southern desert border of Israel as promised by the God of Abraham, Isaac and Jacob to Israel. And, of course, God's southern border for Israel also provides the solution to the Islamic threat, which is to terminate Islam. But to terminate Islam, one must "capture the flag", or the Ka'abah in Mecca and either raise the Israeli flag over it or remove it as the vortex of Islam's evil system. Cut off the head of the snake, and the crushing and seemingly undefeatable coils that are then released and removed from around the human race.

At a time in which many believe that Islam's march to victory is unstoppable, I believe that Islam can be stopped and terminated with one swift blow. We have no choice. Without

Mecca and Medina under Islamic control, there can be no Islam anywhere else in the world because there will then be no more "Hajj" or pilgrimage to Mecca. Hajj represents one of the five pillars of Islam. Remove that pillar and the whole edifice collapses because just as Jerusalem is the city of the God of Abraham, Isaac and Jacob, Mecca is the city of Allah, Ishmael and Mohammed. And there is no choice for the human race but to terminate the Islamic menace by taking control of Mecca and Medina. Ultimately, the Moslems themselves will be blessed when they realize that their worse-than-Nazi system has been defeated, and they are forced to embrace Western Civilization and Democracy. This book does not call for the West to invade Saudi Arabia, but it does educate the world to understand why this will happen inevitably through the internal anarchy brought about by the "Arab Spring", and the resulting collapse of the Saudi kingdom. I believe God's justification for this will be the defeat of Allah by God and victory of Jerusalem over the Moslem "holy cities."

Democracy and the blessings of Western Civilization could not be brought to the people of Germany, Japan and Italy until the Nazi/Tojo/Fascist systems were utterly defeated militarily. Though the nuclear bombings at Hiroshima and Nagasaki were a tragedy, ultimately they ended WWII immediately and brought peace and blessings to the Japanese people, who are a good people. So are the Germans and Italians good people. So are the Moslems good people. But the Islamic system must be defeated once and for all to bless the Moslems and the entire human race or all of humanity and the planet Earth will be destroyed by Islam.

Just as the Moslems say there will be no peace in the Middle East without the Moslems getting Jerusalem, so, too, I say, there will be no peace in the Middle East or on Earth until the Jews and Christians get Mecca and Medina, and God is declared the victor over the pagan Allah al-Ilahi, the moon-god, war-god and sword-god commonly understood by me and many other people to be Satan.

Allahu Akbar does not mean: God is great. What it means is that Allah is GREATER than the God of the Jews and the Christians. According to Christian theology, which, by the way, is derived from Judaism, this was the reason for the expulsion of Satan, Lucifer, the Devil from God's court and Satan's resulting hatred for all humans created in God's image. My sixth book: Return to Mecca signaled the final victory of God and the Human Race by the West putting an end to this destructive call of death of Allahu Akbar that Satan is greater.

After completing *"Return to Mecca,"* and self-publishing it in April, 2012, I was fairly satisfied that I would not be writing any more books, because I was looking forward to stopping my endless traveling abroad, which is what I needed to promote my newly written books, and staying home in Israel to form and lead the Bible Bloc Party in Israel's Knesset elections and then get elected to the Knesset at the head of this Judeo-Christian Western Civilization party. And of course, one cannot get elected without a campaign which requires that I stay home in Israel!

But a number of things happened which forced me to change my mind about not writing any more new books and obliging myself to write, publish and continue traveling overseas albeit for a short time.

Although *"Return to Mecca"* was written already well into the "Arab Spring" which began in February 2011, and although my wife, Rachel, whose job it is to monitor the Arabic language broadcasts of our neighbors, already knew about the nascent ISIS, ISIL, or IS at that time, it wasn't until 2014 that the Islamic caliphate was declared showing the world the ferociousness of this organization – something totally in keeping with Saudi governance and methods within the Kingdom of Saudi Arabia, the founder of all of these Sunni terrorist organizations: Al-Qaeda, Jaba'at al Nusra, Hamas, Islamic Jihad, Khorosan, the Salafists, and many other organizations all based on fanatic, pure, pristine, Islamic evil. My sixth book dealt primarily with biblical scripture pointing to the return of the Jews to Arabia, and land where our feet tread, and therefore was promised to us in the Book of Deuteronomy. Even the Arabs and the Kurds know this land will be taken by the Jews according to God's word. This book deals more with the military, political and economic aspects of the fall of Mecca to Judeo-Christian Western Civilization and Democracy.

The second issue which needed mentioning was the Ukrainian revolution of February, 2014, in which the pro-Russian president Yanukovich of that time was overthrown by Ukrainian nationalists and a new president, Petro Poroshenko, was elected. These Ukrainian nationalists' policies were repugnant to the Russian ethnic minorities in the eastern part of Ukraine. Actually, since the creation of independent Ukraine, the trend was for the Ukrainians to force ethnic Russian citizens not to speak Russian but Ukrainian. This led to a civil war today between the Ukrainian government and military vs. the Russian backed separatists in the East.

A third issue is the updated situation of Iran's nuclear as well as terrorist activities throughout the Middle East as well as in other parts of the world which are all leading up to a confrontation between Shi'ite and Sunni Islam over who exactly will be preeminent in the Islamic world.

This struggle between Shi'ite Iran and Sunni Saudi

Arabia, both sides of which are fanatic and evil, will be consummated in the final battle over Mecca, the holy city of all Moslems. This reality provides us with more pieces of the jigsaw puzzle as to how Mecca eventually will be the final battle site between Shi'ites and Sunnis, followed by the One World Government intervention, followed by Israel's entry into the fray at the orders of the One World Government followed by the defeat of Islam in its entirety followed by the one and a half billion Moslems embracing the God of Abraham, Isaac, and Jacob.

For all these above reasons, I felt that this seventh book would clarify aspects not dealt with in "Return to Mecca" which was a book based more on Bible prophecy and scholarship rather than economic, military and political issues.

CHAPTER I

AMERICAN POLICY FALLACIES

There is a saying: "It takes a thief to know a thief." I believe this applies aptly to the inability of most Jews and Christians to understand Islam, and therefore policy decisions, both in Christian countries as well as Israel are often based on fallacies and an inability to understand the *real* challenges facing a Western Civilization and Democracy political system. This applies both to the Western democratic countries as well as Jewish Israel.

America was founded in 1620 as a refuge of loyal, English, Protestant and later European Christians seeking the freedom of religion as well as the freedom to grow, develop and build new lives in the newly discovered territories of the North American continent which seemed to be a territory with unlimited wealth and potential.

In the 1820's and 1830's, famous French author and historian Alexis De Tocqueville summarized the American people as follows (to paraphrase President Dwight D. Eisenhower's summary of De Tocqueville's book: Democracy in America):

"America will be the greatest country on Earth because the American people are a good people, and their pulpits are on fire for the Lord." Conversely, Eisenhower continues: *"America will lose its pre-eminence in the world when*

American pulpits are no longer on fire for the Lord." May this serve as a wise warning to the American people!

German philosopher Heinrich Heine also said about the same time, two hundred years ago: *"The world is going to have to choose between the foolishness of the Americans and the despotism and tyranny of the Russians."*

So, the *"goodness"* of the Americans is intermixed with the *"foolishness"* of the Americans.

When I am in churches and synagogues in the US, Canada and Europe I warn the good people coming to hear me that the US has been world power number one for over a hundred years because, even though they are *"foolish"*, they are *"foolish in the Lord."* Both in Proverbs and the New Testament it says that the foolishness of the Lord is greater than the wisdom of man.

Therefore, my conclusion has always been that as long as a country believes in God; the God of Abraham, Isaac and Jacob, it is foolish in the Lord, but is blessed by God and attains pre-eminence. But once a nation abandons God, they are no longer *"foolish in the Lord,"* but simply foolish which is what seems to be happening today in Obama's America.

In World War II, British Prime Minister Winston Churchill was reputed to have said: *"America always does the right thing... after it has exhausted all the other possible alternatives."* And indeed, in WWII, The United States of America made many mistakes but came out on top because America was foolish, but it was foolish in the Lord.

Now, regarding Islam, America really was not very interested in Islam and lived in a very prophylactic isolationist world by developing itself, firstly within the original 13 colonies that were part of the British Crown, but then later expanded by absorbing new territories until it reached 50 states at present. From my 66 years of life and experience, I see that most Americans are very satisfied and self-satisfied in the richest country of the world and don't really take much of an interest in anything happening outside its borders. People don't even know the names of the Mexican president or Canadian prime minister next door.

America's exposure to Islam really began with this nasty habit of the North African Berbers and Arabs of hijacking American merchant ships and taking American sailors irrevocably as slaves with no hope of freedom and redemption.

Then American ambassador to Paris, France, Benjamin Franklin tried his best to negotiate the freedom of these high demand American sailor slaves but to no avail. No amount of money could serve as a ransom to redeem these slaves.

President Thomas Jefferson therefore decided to read the Koran, the book of Islam, to understand the *"nature of the beast."* Based on the horrible things written in the Koran, President Jefferson decided to build a naval fleet – what was to become the US Navy, and created a specialized branch of commandos which became the US Marines.

In 1803, this brand new navy and unit of Marines went to war with the Barbary Pirates and only through the use of the sword were the Americans able to free these enslaved merchant sailors. The outcome of this war was an agreement that the Barbary Pirates would no longer take American sailors as prisoners and sell them into slavery.

Ironically, US media incorrectly says that President Jefferson was a *"true"* liberal by reading the Koran, and that's why Moslem Congressman Keith Ellison of Minneapolis, Minnesota swore his oath in Congress on Jefferson's copy of the Koran. But the truth is that Jefferson was indeed open to reading the Koran, but did so in order to understand the nature of the Islamic slavery beast, and afterwards was motivated to build a navy and a military unit known as the US Marines to go into battle with the Moslems and terminate the threat to US Naval and Merchant Marine vessels.

It's kind of like saying, *"I read Hitler's 'Mein Kampf' book so I am a true liberal after agreeing with what it says."* That is perhaps the first fallacy of American thinking. It takes a thief to know a thief. Americans, Jews or Christians, go by a certain system and therefore are unable to understand an antithetical evil system known as Islam, which calls for the death of the Jews on Saturday and Christians on Sunday (Hadith Bukhari and Sahih Muslim).

My personal life story is that I moved to Israel in 1968 and kind of felt like *"Lawrence of Arabia"* returning home to Israel. My mother, of blessed memory, always jokingly said: *"You're not Lawrence of Arabia. You are Avi of the Negev,"* (southern Israel.)

When I met Rachel, my wife to be, I believe I was attracted to her for a number of reasons, one of them that she was beautiful, another that she was a good cook, but also because she immediately went to work to rid me of the fallacies of my American thinking towards the Middle East, the Arabs and Islam.

Interestingly enough, the 1803 war with the Barbary Pirates terminated the taking of American citizens and sailors as slaves, but not British citizens and sailors, and so, the British, in turn went to war with the Moroccans and other Barbary Pirates in 1817 extracting a similar agreement. The point was made.

In my opinion one of the reasons for the French colonization of North Africa (Morocco, Algeria and Tunisia) was indeed the piracy threatening France from the South. The East-West French colonization in Africa then went into sub-Saharan Africa as well, while the British sought to colonize African nations from North to South, from Egypt to South Africa.

The Italians also looked southward and took Libya as their colony. Only through military occupation of North Africa could Europe rid itself of this horrible slavery and banditry of Islam. It is interesting that today, ISIL (Islamic State in Levant) seeks to use Libya as a springboard to counter-attack and take vengeance upon Italy and the Vatican in Rome. We mustn't forget that the Arabs were at the gates of Rome in 868 AD/CE and would only desist from sacking Rome if the Vatican paid a great ransom in gold. Gold will not help this time. This is another reason for the fall and banning of Islam: The world cannot tolerate this crazy Islamic behavior any more of turning the Vatican into a mosque and Europe into part of the Caliphate.

And Spain fought a war of *"Reconquista"* (re-conquest of the Iberian Peninsula) from 711 to 1492, defeating Islam. Spain secured a few miniscule colonies in Morocco: Tangiers, Ceuta and Melilla. Tangiers was restored to Morocco as part of de-colonization.

Matamoros is a Mexican city on the border with Brownsville, Texas. Most Mexicans and Americans are clueless that the name Matamoros means: *"Moor-killers"* (Moroccans or Moslems). All of this originates with this 781 year war between the Spanish and the Moslem Moroccans.

After the United Nations conducted its de-colonization program in the 20th century, this all led to independence for these Moslem nations, the restoration of piracy and slavery, and again a threat to Christian Western Civilization from those lands south of Europe. Europe is also inundated with Moslem migrants coming to work in Europe but refusing to assimilate and integrate with the Christians, but yes wish to conquer Europe and Islamicize it for the *"glory of Allah."*

There were two powerful reasons for Europe's invitation of this Islamic invasion: The promise by the Arabs of stable oil supplies after the 1973 war between Israel and the Arabs resulting in an oil sales embargo on Europe by the Arabs. And secondly, according to my Christian friends in Europe; the Europeans aborted 50 million Christian babies, and so God rewarded them with 50 million Moslem immigrants to provide labor for European industries. Now, it seems the Europeans are stuck with a ticking time bomb of Islamic population in the heart of every Christian European nation.

Now, returning to the United States of America— throughout the 19th century and early 20th century, exposure to the threat of Islam was a very distant thing going all the way back to 1803, and very tangential unless seen in the prism of oil exploration and world coalitions seeking to attain this oil, and later financial benefits accruing from oil exploration by Western *"Christian"* oil companies and exploration.

After World War I and the dismemberment of the Ottoman Turkish Empire, British and American oil interests began to become interested in Saudi Arabia with the first oil exploration efforts beginning in 1927. It must be remembered that the United States was self-sufficient in petroleum at that time and true interest in Islamic countries only began with the Saudis "striking it rich" with the successful oil drilling in the late 1920's and thereafter.

True, the Saudis had a very strong, traditional, Islamic system, incompatible really with Western values, but for the sake of good business, the British and Americans swallowed their pride and values, and agreed to do whatever was necessary to attain incredible oil wealth. This later was to happen, of course, in other Islamic lands as well such as Libya, Algeria, Iran and Iraq, amongst others.

But, what clearly served as a catalyst for the West's total

ideological capitulation to Islamic countries for the sake of oil interests was the rise of Adolf Hitler's Nazism in 1933, followed by World War II in 1939.

Nazi Germany, a great industrial power, possessed very little petroleum of its own and needed to import or confiscate oil from other countries it conquered during WWII such as the Ploesti fields in Romania. Germany also tried, in its conquest of the Soviet Union, to reach the oil fields in Azerbaijan, but they were successfully blocked by the Red Army.

It was, therefore, an imperative for the Nazis to reach the oil wells of Saudi Arabia which were under British and American control, even though Saudi Arabia was technically an independent country.

Field-Marshall Irvin von Rommel led the Africa-Corps forces in North Africa with the intention of defeating British Field-Marshall General Montgomery in El-Alamein thus opening the path to the Saudi oil, but the allies, led by Field-Marshall Montgomery were victorious.

An interesting side-note: The Jewish community in the British Mandate of Palestine was preparing for a last ditch battle against Rommel's forces in Palestine with cyanide pills ready to be handed out to the Jewish inhabitants should the Nazis have won.

From the Moslem perspective, it must be stressed that ideologically, the Arabs/Moslems had much more in common with the Nazi ideology rather than with the Anglo-Saxon British/American ideology of democracy.

So, for example, Turkey was an ally of Kaiser Wilhelm's Germany in WWI, and Iran was divided up by British and Russian spheres of influence, because the Iranians also felt a closeness with and admiration of Germany both in WWI and WWII.

In WWII, this time, Iran was divided up into three spheres of influence: American, British and Soviet out of fears that Iran, like Turkey would have pro-German, pro-Nazi, tendencies though Turkey actually remained neutral in WWII.

One of the reasons today for Iranian antagonism against the US was because in 1952, the US government overthrew the democratically elected government of the nationalist and very popular leader Mosadegh out of fears that Iran would get closer to the USSR and would have too independent a foreign policy. The US then installed the Shah Reza Pahlavi instead of Mosadegh, incurring a lingering resentment from many Iranians leading eventually to his downfall in 1979.

Indeed, another fallacy of US policy and decision-making was the then-overthrow of the Shah in 1979 by then-President Jimmy Carter and his advisor, Zbigniew Brzhezhinski. Jimmy Carter mistakenly believed that Ayatollah Khomeini was a *"man of God"* just as Jimmy Carter was; that they could work together, and that Khomeini would unite the people of Iran whereas the Shah was a *"violator of human rights,"* being a dictator. Look what Khomeini and the Ayatollahs did to human rights since 1979!!! I will talk more about this in Chapter III. A man of God and a man of Allah are not one in the same, but opposites, because the God of the Jews and Christians; the God of Abraham, Isaac and Jacob, is the opposite of Allah al-Ilahi, the moon-god, war-god and sword god—which is Satan.

But returning to the Islamic tendency to favor the Nazis over the democratic nations, the infamous Moslem Brotherhood was founded in Egypt by Hassan al-Banna in 1929 as a fanatic religious movement bent on the overthrowing the British domination and occupation of Egypt at that time and was promptly banned by the British authorities in Egypt. The Moslem Brotherhood wished to impose fanatic Shariah law in Egypt and saw itself clearly as an ally of the Nazis after 1933 and hoped and prayed that the Nazis would be victorious in defeating the British. Also, the Arab approach was: *"The enemy of my enemy is my ally."* This could be seen not only in Egypt, but in the British mandates of Palestine and Iraq. The common bottom line of both Islam and Nazism is the eradication of the Jews on Saturday and the Christians on Sunday.

Great efforts were made by both the British and the Americans during the North African campaigns to placate the Moslems/Arabs at *any* cost to ensure their loyalty and submission to the allied cause. Former president of Egypt, Anwar Sadat, who actually made peace with Israel in 1979, was a convicted Nazi supporter in WWII and jailed by the British.

At this point, I would like to share a testimony, the only testimony, in all six of my previous books, regarding an experience I had in Dallas, Texas in April of 1991 which helps to clarify the duplicitous role of the Allies in World War II, in being accomplices to the deaths of six million Jews in the Nazi Holocaust.

I had just been illegally fired because of my right-wing political views by left-wing bureaucrats at the Government Press Office, part of the Prime Minister's Office during Yitzhak Shamir's tenure from January 1989 to October 1990. Even though Prime Minister Yitzhak Shamir was the leader of the right-wing conservative Likud Party, the civil service was still solidly controlled by the left-wing Labor Party—something in effect since 1922.

Even though I was eventually cleared of the lies placed in my personnel file through the direct intervention of former Ambassador Yoram Ettinger, who was the director and my first boss in the Government Press Office, it became clear to me that I could not go back to the News Department and needed to look for another form of employment.

I had been corresponding with Nancy, a Christian Evangelical from New Braunfels, Texas, over a period of five years, and she convinced me to come over to the US and she would open doors for me in churches, synagogues, messianic groups, radio and TV. She indeed kept her word and that was how I started my new career as a speaker. God had to hermetically close the doors for me in Israel to open the doors in the US, Canada and Europe. I also felt like Joseph who was expelled from Canaan by his brothers, but later became viceroy to Pharaoh in Egypt, all by God's plan. Perhaps the **Bible Bloc/Gush Hatanakhi Party** will be the path by which I return to Israel and fulfill a destiny higher than I would have ever imagined.

My first visit to the US as a speaker was in November and December of 1990, at the height of Desert Shield; the preparatory buildup before Operation Desert Storm. Everywhere I went, I spoke of what was about to happen in Kuwait based on information from briefings with our superior officers in the IDF (Israel Defense Forces) as a spokesman in the IDF reserves.

During that visit, I also had the opportunity to speak and participate in religious services at the Conservative Agudas Achim synagogue in San Antonio, at the invitation of Rabbi Richard Spiegel. I was asked to speak about the military realities on the eve of Desert Storm, and was well received by the congregation.

A Jewish woman attending the Bar Mitzvah celebration in the synagogue that Sabbath was from Dallas and told me she was a PR woman and could get me to speak before the Dallas Council on World Affairs, one of the most important political-economic forums in the US.

Indeed, after returning to Israel and being with my wife and kids during Desert Storm (January-March 1991), I returned to New York and received an urgent call from this PR lady who told me to get on the next flight to Dallas because there was a sudden opening for me to speak before the Dallas Council on World Affairs.

Upon arrival at the Stouffer Hotel in Dallas (now Renaissance), I was greeted by Gen. Latham (ret.), head of the Dallas Council, who explained to me that usually, their meetings are planned a year or two in advance, but because of a no-show, they needed a speaker immediately for someone who gave two lectures out of four, but had called in sick and could not appear.

That speaker was President Boris Yeltsin of Russia! He was a severe alcoholic, and had a drink which was enough to get him onto a plane back to a sanatorium in Russia!

So the third night's lecture was a wash-out and I was called in to replace the President of Russia on the fourth night! God had to make Boris Yeltsin drunk so that the doors would open for Avi Lipkin to replace him! This was just after the Jewish holy day of Purim, so drunkenness was an ironic reason for the door to open for me, but God has a sense of humor.

In addition, God had another trick up His sleeve. When I arrived at the hotel to speak, General Latham asked me: *"So what's it like to be a GENERAL in the Israeli army?"*

"General?" I responded.

"Aren't you General A. Lipkin, chief-of-staff of the Israeli army?"

(He thought he was getting General Amnon Lipkin-Shahak, then chief-of-staff of the Israeli army!)

I answered, *"No, I am Lieutenant A. Lipkin of the IDF*

25

Spokesman's Office in the reserves."

It seems that for some people in Dallas, Amnon and Avi are all the same!

So God tricked the Dallas Council people into thinking they got the IDF chief-of-staff. Instead they got Lieutenant (res.) A. Lipkin of the Army Spokesman's Office. But God has his reasons!

Latham was livid! But realizing the crowd of dignitaries was waiting for my speech, he told me: *"You'd better do a good job!"*

And I did. They even invited me back for another meeting, but the Israeli government vetoed the meeting because it would have been a dialogue with PLO representative in the US, Professor Edward Said. The Israeli Embassy in Washington told me I couldn't talk to PLO terrorists! All this was against the backdrop of secret Israeli-PLO meetings in Oslo in preparation for the disaster known as the so-called Oslo Peace Process. Such important people as Yitzhak Rabin, Shimon Peres and Yossi Beilin were meeting with PLO terrorist representatives at that same time.

General Latham warned me: *"No politics. We want only a military spokesman's presentation, please!"*

And so that is what I did.

A few words about the people attending this meeting of the Dallas Council on World Affairs: These people are among the richest, most powerful and most influential in the United States of America and perhaps the entire world. They included bankers, corporation leaders, ranchers and there were also quite a few Moslem dignitaries at my lecture.

This meeting which took place in April, 1991, was attended primarily by supporters of then-President, George Herbert Walker Bush, and then-Secretary of State, James Baker III, both of whom were notoriously anti-Shamir if not anti-Israel. I realized I was not in a friendly setting.

So I did my best to present a professional military message from Israel's perspective. Since this was a tie and jacket affair, and these people looked like they were dressed in their *"Sunday best"* for church, I mistakenly thought they were Christian church-goers and therefore I tried to use examples from the Bible to make my point.

I told them: *"Jesus of Nazareth would walk down from Nazareth to the Sea of Galilee – to Capernaum where he met the fishermen. That was a few hours of walking, which tourists and pilgrims can do along what is known today as the Jesus Trail. Indeed you see the Sea of Galilee from the eastern outskirts of Nazareth."*

"From there, Jesus walked southward along the Jordan River to Jericho where he was baptized in the Jordan River with John the Baptist. Then, after baptism, he walked up to Jerusalem in about five hours where he then served at the Temple on Mt. Moriah."

"Israel is a small country," I explained. *"One can drive from the Mediterranean Sea to the Dead Sea in one hour and fifteen minutes, kind of like from Dallas to Ft. Worth! One can hike from Jericho and the Jordan River border to Jerusalem in five hours. Arab or Islamic armies can do it in less. It only takes twenty minutes to drive from the Jordan River to Jerusalem, whether it is in a private vehicle, a tank or a half-track."*

"Jordanian Air Force pilots can take off from Amman Airport and bomb Jerusalem in three minutes, go on to bomb Tel-Aviv in three more minutes and then be back in Amman sipping Turkish coffee in five minutes."

"The US Air Force has eleven minutes scramble time. Arab pilots can take off, bomb Jerusalem and Tel-Aviv and be back at their bases in eleven minutes. We don't have 11

minutes scramble time. That's how small Israel is."

"And if we give up control over the Jordan River, there is no way of stopping a million-man or ten-million-man march to the Mediterranean Sea of Islamic volunteers. It would be like a Chinese or North Korean human wave assault during the Korean War. There is no weapon that could stop that."

So my explanation stressed the three strategies: infantry, mechanized units, and air force attacks on Israel.

I explained that withdrawing from the Golan Heights would allow the Syrian military to take Tiberias in 15 minutes, Safed in 30 and Haifa in one hour.

Gaza could not be handed over because it would be like the Dutch boy pulling his finger out of the dike. (Indeed we did hand over Gaza, and did we get peace? We got the opposite, and we have had to return to Gaza a number of times to deal with rockets, mortars and terrorist tunnels. And we will probably have to return to Gaza again to terminate the Hamas mis-rule once and for all.)

I concluded by telling these people that Israel wants peace. All governments of Israel want peace. Former Prime Minister Yitzhak Rabin handed over half the Golan to Syria in 1974 as a result of then secretary-of-state Henry Kissinger's disengagement talks. This was 2% of the land Israel was forced to take in wars of self-defense in 1967 and 1973. Former Prime Minister Menahem Begin handed over the Sinai Peninsula to Egypt a third time in 1981, for a peace agreement with Egypt. Sinai represented 91% of the lands Israel was forced to take in the Six Day War in 1967 and the Yom Kippur War in 1973.

My point was that between the Golan and Sinai, Israel had already returned 93% of the lands it was forced to take in wars imposed on Israel by the Arab nations surrounding Israel. Israel had fulfilled 93% of UN Resolutions 242 and

338 calling on Israel to hand over land for peace, but the same UN resolutions said that Israel would negotiate with its neighbors for new borders which were *"secure, recognized and defensible,"* the inference being that Israel was not to hand over all the lands it took in wars of self-defense, because then it would be contrary to the UN resolutions calling for *"borders that were secure, recognized and defensible."* Clearly, the 1967 borders were not secure, recognized and defensible. The US Joint Chiefs-of-Staff said that Israel could not possibly defend itself in the June 5th, 1967 borders. Kissinger called these borders Auschwitz Extermination Camp borders.

So this was my message.

After I spoke, we adjourned to a smaller room where I met with senior members of the Dallas Council on World Affairs. What they told me was shocking and perhaps the most important message I ever received in these three decades of lectures. Now they laid the law down for me as if I were prime minister of Israel, or at least indeed, the chief-of-staff. I think I can now understand what Israeli leaders are told when they visit the US.

They opened with some flattery followed by threats.

"Avi," they said, *"you are good speaker for Israel because you are an American-born Jew and you don't speak with a 'funny' Israeli accent. Here in Dallas, TX, we don't like 'funny accents'. We don't like Russian accents* (Yeltsin), *Arabic accents* (VIP Oil Princes), *we don't like Israeli accents, and we don't even like Queen's English from Oxford. And you speak like a Yankee* (Northerner), *but you speak clear English and it is easy for us to understand you. But your problem is you don't know realities. We of the Dallas Council on World Affairs are going to teach you realities:*

"Reality #1: Israel is all alone. America is tired of

29

paying for Israel's wars. We gave you an airlift in 1973 during the Yom Kippur War. Without that, Israel would have lost. America is not your ally any more. You Jews are all alone. You Jews are going to make peace with the Arabs whether you like it or not. And you are not going to give them 91% or 93% of the lands taken in 1967 and 1973. You will return 100% of the lands—the whole 9 yards and more than a 100%. And we don't even care about UN resolutions 242 and 338 giving you new borders which are secure recognized and defensible."

"Reality #2: There is only one thing that made America great, and that is the barrel of oil—the steady price and steady supply of oil, and we won't let the Jews get in the way of that. Is that clear?"

Now I was in total shock, and before I could answer them, one of my Christian dinner guests, Eric Gustavson, who a few months before had arranged for me to appear on the Zola Levitt TV program as well as the Marlin Maddoux *"Point of View"* radio show in Dallas, stood up shaking, and with my permission and the permission of the Dallas Council addressed the audience saying: *"You call yourselves Christians? You say that what made America great was the barrel of oil? You should be ashamed of yourselves! What made America great was not the barrel of oil. What made America great was Jesus Christ!"*

At this point it finally dawned on me that there are two types of Americans: Christians who love Israel and Americans who love mammon, money and oil. The lights went on. I knew I had to choose between the two. I chose aligning myself with the Christians who loved Israel and the Jews and blessed Israel.

Then Eric's daughter, Carol Burton, arose, and said: *"And it says in the Bible: 'I will bless those who bless you*

(Israel) *and curse those who curse you!'"* (Gen. 12:3).

Had America had a Christian, Bible-believing, president in WWII, instead of the Socialist Democrat, Franklin Delano Roosevelt, we might have been able to save a few million of the otherwise-doomed Jews of Europe. Even towards the end of WWII, after the death of Roosevelt, then-President Harry Truman could have sent a B-17 or a British Lancaster bomber to destroy a railroad track or bridge therefore stopping the deaths of tens of thousands of Jews a day in the gas chambers and ovens. It would not have negatively affected the outcome of the war. But the decision was *intentionally* made to allow the industrial killing of the Jews. There was an agenda to kill the Jews, or allow them to be killed in the Holocaust, all for the sake of oil and placating the Arabs who had the allies *"over a barrel!"*

Finally, I gathered up my gumption and responded: *"Israel and Jews have never come in the way of America's steady oil supplies and prices. In fact, we lost six million Jews in WWII in order for America to maintain steady oil prices and supplies. And if you think we will sacrifice ourselves again in another Holocaust, we will not!"*

What came to mind was the German refugee ship, the St. Louis, which departed from the German port of Hamburg in May 1939, en route to Havana, Cuba, carrying 900 German Jews—the crème de la crème of German Jewry. They had valid German passports as well as valid immigration visas to Cuba, but US Assistant Secretary of State, in charge of visas, Breckinridge Long, called the Cuban Government and told them to cancel the visas and send the ship back to Germany.

On its way back to Europe, the St. Louis stopped in three different places off the coast of Florida trying to dislodge its passengers, but the US State Department refused to allow these miserable, doomed people off the ship, and the US

31

Coast Guard encircled the boat to ensure that no one jumped ship and swam to shore.

The US would not take in these German Jews. Then the ship sailed northward past the Canadian Maritime Provinces, and hundreds of pastors signed a petition begging former prime minister McKenzie King for mercy for these people. They begged that at least the children be allowed to disembark, but McKenzie King's response was: *"One Jew was one Jew too many."* There was no mercy even for the Jewish children on board that ship.

The St. Louis returned to Europe allowing the Jews to disembark in the Belgian port of Antwerp after WWII had broken out but before the Wehrmacht had conquered Belgium. Out of the 900 passengers, 800 died in the Holocaust. Only 100 survived.

All of this for America's oil supplies. And now the people of the Dallas Council on World Affairs were saying to me that the Jews of Israel would also be sacrificed on the altar of oil.

But it's not only the Jews being sacrificed for the barrel of oil. Millions of Blacks in Africa have been killed, tortured, and enslaved by the Moslems. They never heard of President Abraham Lincoln's Emancipation Proclamation of 1863. They never heard of the Marines *"to the shores of Tripoli."* It's just fine if the Moslems have the oil, the money, and the numbers influencing US and World politics. Money and petroleum take precedence over the lives of Jews, Christians and African Blacks.

Then, we saw the collapse of Yugoslavia in 1990-1991. Then, it was thousands of Christians, primarily Serbs, who were slaughtered by the Bosnian and Albanian Moslems. Even NATO participated in the slaughter of the Christians by ruthless air bombardment by NATO aircraft. There are now three Moslem countries in the heart of Europe: Bosnia, Kosovo, and Albania, with Macedonia approaching 40% Albanian population—and itself soon to become a Moslem nation. All of this at the behest of Moslem petrodollars and influence. So Jews, Blacks in Africa, and Christians in Yugoslavia may be sacrificed to the Moslem sword. Do we forget the island of East Timor, where 500,000 Catholics were killed by Indonesian Moslems until the UN and Australia finally intervened to give East Timor independence and stop the genocide by the Moslems?

Here's another example: Half a million Chinese died in Indonesia in the 1960's. The Western media described these Chinese as Communists from Mainland China. No, these people were family business people and not Communists. But Indonesia has oil—the Holy Grail of the world economic system. So the Chinese were sacrificed as well, slaughtered by the Moslem Indonesians. The Chinese also have a collective memory.

After World War II, there was a quantum shift. The enemy was no longer Nazi Germany or Tojo Japan. The enemy now was Soviet Communism. Former US Secretary-of-State, George Marshall, vehemently opposed the establishment of the State of Israel—even after the deaths of six million Jews in the Holocaust! And that was because he didn't want to alienate the Arab and Islamic world, which again was perceived as essential in the Cold War with Russia and China.

In 1956, Egyptian President Gamal Abdul Nasser, shut the straights of Tiran at the southern tip of the Sinai Peninsula to Israeli shipping. This was a *casus belli*, or a cause of war with Israel, because international law stipulates that the blockading of an international waterway by one country against another country is a cause for war. The Gulf of Aqaba is bordered by four nations: Israel, Jordan, Saudi Arabia and Egypt. If Egypt places its heavy artillery at the southern tip of the Sinai Peninsula to bombard any Israeli ship passing by the Straits of Tiran, it is a cause of war. Egypt was also massing its troops on the border of Israel and fedayeen or terrorists were infiltrating into Israel and causing much death and destruction, so Israel undertook the Sinai Campaign in 1956 to open up the Straits of Tiran.

At the same time, the Suez Canal, owned by the British and French who built it, was nationalized by Abdul Nasser, so the tripartite alliance of Israel, France and Britain, attacked Egypt to remove the blockades of the Straits of Tiran and the nationalization of the Suez Canal by Egypt and restore the *status quo ante.*

During the negotiations for the withdrawal of Israeli troops from the Straits of Tiran and Sinai, President Dwight D. Eisenhower promised the Israelis that in return for Israel's withdrawal, the US Six Fleet would guarantee that the straits would never again be blockaded by the Egyptians or anyone else, and if that indeed happened, the US Sixth Fleet would intervene and re-open the straits for Israeli shipping.

When indeed in 1967, the Egyptians again blockaded the Straits of Tiran, and Israel produced its copy of Eisenhower's promise, the State Department took three weeks to *"look for its copy"* in the State Department's vaults, and *"couldn't find it."* The result was the Six Day War on June 5th, 1967 after US promises were not kept. The US could not be counted on to defend Israel even if it gave its solemn word and guarantee. This lesson has been learned and is in effect to this day.

Not only that, after three days of the Six Day War, Israel had completed its victory in Sinai and pulled its troops out of Sinai to fight the Jordanians in Jerusalem and the West Bank, leaving Sinai virtually without any Israeli soldiers in place. The infamous "USS Liberty affair" took place when it became clear that the NSA spy ship was stabbing Israel in the back by telling the Egyptians: *No Israeli soldiers in Sinai. Now, Egypt can easily take it back."* The USS Liberty was strafed by Israeli Air Force jets resulting in the deaths of 22 US sailors, a tragic outcome indeed.

Then-President Lyndon Baines Johnson, claimed ignorance of the affair and said that the USS Liberty should have been sunk for its treachery to Israel.

Israel did apologize and did pay reparations for the strafing. Israel could have easily sunk the ship, but merely wanted to send a message warning the US of duplicity, supposedly being Israel's ally and then behaving in a treasonous manner by revealing top Israeli secret information to the Egyptian enemy.

During the 1973 Yom Kippur War and during the days leading up to it, Israel was suffering from a term known as *"the concept."* The concept, amongst Israel's top military and political echelons, was that the Arabs were not going to attack Israel. It was inconceivable for Israel's top Socialist Labor Party people ruling Israel to believe that the Arabs would dare to attack across the Suez Canal as well as along the Golan Heights.

Israeli intelligence officers saw it coming. Their reports were rebuffed by the Socialist leadership of Israel. Israel had a spy in Egypt warning of the approaching conflict. King Hussein of Jordan warned then Israeli Prime Minister Golda Meir that a war was in the offing, and the Israeli leadership was led by astray by head of the Military Intelligence General Zeira who suffered from the concept that the Arabs would never attack all mighty Israel.

Former US Secretary of State Henry Kissinger even knew about the war, but did not make an effort to warn Israel.

Israel paid dearly with over 2,700 deaths of its soldiers and a similar number of critically injured.

It was at this time that, to his credit, that then-President Richard Nixon provided Israel with an airlift that saved Israel. Half of Israel's aircraft were downed by Soviet anti-aircraft missiles which had been placed in areas which by agreement were to be demilitarized, and half of Israel's tanks were destroyed by Soviet produced anti-tank rockets.

Israel, after initial failures, reversed the course of the war and crossed the Suez Canal into the heart of Egypt encircling the Egyptian 2nd and 3rd Armies. The Soviets then started to mobilize to intervene on behalf of Egypt and that's when the US and the World forced Israel into a ceasefire and then into withdrawing from Egypt and then to withdraw completely from the Sinai Peninsula. Israel compromised 91% by returning Sinai to Egypt and compromised 2% by returning half the Golan to Syria in 1974. So isn't it logical that the Arabs compromise 7% for peace? That's what the Arabs signed on to.

Israel won the war, but lost the subsequent peace.

Now the Arabs and world governments demand that Israel withdraw from 100% of the lands Israel was forced to take in wars of self-defense and return to indefensible borders, something contrary to UN Resolutions 242 and 338 calling for a 7% compromise by the Arabs.

On the flip side of the coin, from that time on, Israel has gone over almost entirely to using American made jet aircraft, tanks, artillery, as well as other US produced war materiel. The American military and people since 1973 have been generous. The alliance with the US military has become solidified.

At the same time, a peace agreement subsequently was signed on the White House lawn in 1979 between President

Anwar Sadat of Egypt and Prime Minister Menahem Begin after a difficult negotiating period under the auspices of then-President Jimmy Carter.

Very few people believed that the peace agreement with Egypt would last, but it indeed survived the assassination of then-President Anwar Sadat, thirty years of President Hosni Mubarak and even one year of the Moslem Brotherhood government under then-President Morsi.

It became much stronger, ironically with overthrow of the Moslem Brotherhood President Morsi and the rise of General Abdul-Fattah Al-Sisi, since the fanatic Islam of the Moslem Brotherhood became a common threat both to Israel and Egypt. It seems strange that President Obama is a staunch supporter of the Moslem Brotherhood (and as some claim, a member).

In 1981, the US, under then-President Ronald Reagan, my favorite US president, highly criticized Israel for its successful attack on the nuclear reactor OSIRAK in Iraq, and suspended arms deliveries to Israel for three months. Even Shimon Peres, in behavior typical of the Labor Party, attacked Menahem Begin's attack on OSIRAK instead of acting in a patriotic, unifying national manner. The point here is that the US was opposing Israel's agenda to defend itself from a nuclear threat from Saddam Hussein. But Israel did the world a big favor as could be seen in Desert Storm in 1991 and the invasion of Iraq in 2003. Imagine Saddam Hussein with nuclear weapons!

Another important fallacy of American policy, from the Sunni Arab viewpoint, was the betrayal of the erstwhile ally, Saddam Hussein. Moslems from all over the world look at the betrayal of the Shah of Iran, a Shi'ite, by Jimmy Carter. Then they look at the betrayal of Saddam Hussein by the US after the Iran-Iraq War of 1980-1988.

Iraq purportedly went to war against Iran of Ayatollah Khomeini at the behest of the US and the West to be the defender and shield of the Sunni Arab world and the US in a horrible, bloody war with Shi'ite Iran that took the lives of an estimated one and a half million Iraqis and Iranians.

Iraq emerged bankrupt from this war. And the Iraqis viewed the US as turning its back on Iraq after Iraq fought nine years against the Iranians. The outcome of the war was basically no border changes, but the people died and the economy was destroyed.

Then-American Ambassador, April Gillespie, denies she said it, but the Iraqis claimed she gave Saddam a green light to invade and annex Kuwait to help Iraq pay off its debts. Kuwait had oil and cash that Saddam needed. Saddam claimed Kuwait as a province of Iraq taken away illegally from Iraq after WWI by the British.

Iraq claimed that over 200,000 Iraqis were killed by the US in Desert Storm in the Arab-American alliance's plan to eject Saddam and his forces from Kuwait, something that I believe led to the first attack on the World Trade Center, in February 1993, led by Saddam Hussein agent Ramzi Youssef to punish America with the (failed) toppling of the World Trade Center using a truck bomb underneath the towers.

In my first and third books, I prove this, as well as Saddam Hussein's involvement on April 19th, 1995 in a similar truck bomb attack on the Murrah Federal Building in Oklahoma City, which took 168 lives. Timothy McVeigh and Terry Nichols were disgruntled former US troops in Desert Storm who were trained by Ramzi Youssef founder of the Islamic Abu Sayyaf terrorist group in the Philippines to make these truck bombs.

Similarly, Operation Bojinka, to blow up 12 US civilian airliners taking off from Manila in the Philippines was perpetrated by Ramzi Youssef and TWA 800 was shot down using a Saddam Hussein anti-aircraft missile off the southern shore of Long Island, New York in the summer of 1996, to punish America for its betrayal of Saddam Hussein's loyalty in the war with Iran of 1980-88.

So the US betrayed the Shah of Iran in 1979, the cornerstone of America's cold war in the Mid-East against the Soviets, and then betrayed Saddam Hussein in Desert Storm in 1991 as well as the invasion of Iraq in 2003 to overthrow Saddam Hussein, after the last straw which was the destruction of the two World Trade Center towers on September 11th, 2001. These are two major fallacies of American thinking in the eyes of the Arabs and Moslems. The Moslems say it is better to be an enemy of the US rather than an ally. Look at what America does to its allies!

Returning to US relations with Israel; in 1991, then-President George Herbert Walker Bush also refused to assist Israel in the absorption process of nearly one million immigrants from the former Soviet Union pouring into Israel and providing cheap loans for housing for these immigrants because then-Prime Minister Shamir refused at that time to promote the so-called Oslo peace process which called for the return to the June 5th, 1967 boundaries and the end of settlement activities in Judea, Samaria and Gaza.

In 1998, then-President Bill Clinton forced Israel to hand over 80% of Hebron to the Palestinian Authority, something which caused then-Prime Minister Benjamin Netanyahu, in his first term of office, to fall from power in the 1999 elections.

Clinton even sent James Carville to help Ehud Barak win the elections; a blatant form of foreign US intervention in the Israeli political process, again something we saw happening in the March 17, 2015 Israeli elections. The same efforts were made to again overthrow Prime Minister Benjamin

Netanyahu from power, but back-fired, only increasing Netanyahu's popularity and his success in the polls. And all of this happening with American presidents who claim to be church-going Christians.

At this point, I wish to shift gears into a subject which is rejected by the so-called liberals in the US, primarily lead by the Democrats. It is the Islamic background and faith of President Barack Hussein Obama.

Many dear, good friends of mine in the US are very offended by what I say, but my response to them is: *"You are not married to my wife, Rachel."* (Whose job it has been to listen to and view the Arabic language broadcasts of our neighbors at Kol Israel Radio in Jerusalem, for over 30 years.)

When Rachel began working at Kol Israel as a radio/TV monitor in the Arabic language about 30 years ago, she was astounded to hear what seemed to be a delusional broadcast by the Saudis in which they said: *"Even if it takes us 150 years, we are going to make America a Moslem country."*

Now in 2015, Rachel is picking up broadcasts from the same radio stations saying: *"We thought it was going to take us 150 years to make America a Moslem country, but we were wrong. It's only going to take us 30 years!"*

When then-President George Herbert Walker Bush led the US into Operation Desert Storm, the Saudis were saying: *"We are happy to see America sending its boys and girls to their deaths in Iraq and Afghanistan. They will be our mercenaries. If they defend us as allies, we will provide them with oil, with cash for their economies and be their allies."*

When George W. Bush was president between 2000 and 2008, the Saudis were saying: *"If the US wants to be our ally, they must do what we tell them. If they do so, we will give them oil, cash and support. If they don't we will deny them the oil, the cash and bring down Wall Street."*

On 9/11, 15 of the 19 terrorists who commandeered the four jet airliners which attacked the Twin Trade Towers in NYC, the Pentagon and a fourth jet which went down in Pennsylvania, were Saudis. They weren't poor, but from rich or well-to-do families putting to the lie that terrorists are created because of poverty. They are created because of Islamic Jihad. Saudi Arabia is the first and foremost proponent of Sunni Islamic Jihad. It is part of the problem and not part of the solution.

In 2006, before anyone knew who Mubarak Hussein Obama was, the Saudis announced: *"In the 2008 elections, we will have a Moslem in the White House."* My wife, Rachel, thought the Saudis were delusional. How can the Moslems have a Moslem president in the greatest Christian country of them all – the USA?

It seems there is an agenda. This agenda started long before Obama, long before Clinton, long before the father and son Bush, and going all the way back to Nazi Holocaust of the Jews as I have described earlier in this chapter.

On January 19th, 2010, Rachel was watching what seemed to be an innocent talk show on Channel 3, Cairo TV, called the *Round Table*. Participating in the show were representatives of the Moslem Brotherhood, and their interlocutor was then-Foreign Minister of Egypt, Abu el-Gheit.

They were attacking Abu el-Gheit and President Hosni Mubarak, for treason and betraying Islam, for not breaking the peace treaty with Israel and destroying Israel.

Abu el-Gheit's response was: *"You of the Moslem Brotherhood are like little children. You don't know how to run a country like Egypt and if indeed you were to rule Egypt, you would destroy Egypt."*

"We of the Egyptian government know what we are

41

doing, and know how to rule Egypt and we know what to do with Israel. In fact, let me calm you guys down."

"When US President Obama visited Cairo in 2009, he swore to me that he is a Moslem. His Kenyan father was a Moslem. His Indonesian step-father was a Moslem. He was raised in a mosque and in a madrassa school until age 11, and that he was contending with economic problems as well as Obamacare. But he then said to me that as soon as his economic and Obamacare problems were dealt with, HE WOULD SHOW THE MOSLEM WORLD WHAT HE WOULD DO TO ISRAEL."

Famous Catholic theologian, Francis Xavier is famous for this quote: *"Give me a child until 10 years of age, and I will make him a man."*

Obama was made a Moslem man by age 11. He says so in his auto-biographical books. And indeed, former President of Egypt, Hosni Mubarak, was overthrown after 30 years of virtually dictatorial rule by the Arab Spring uprising in Egypt; though there are reports that the plan for the US to overthrow Mubarak were drawn up during the presidency of Obama's predecessor, George W. Bush who sought to replace Mubarak, according to my sources, for not supporting Bush's plan to attack Iran.

We must also not forget the famous pledge of former president George W. Bush and his Secretary of State, Condoleeza Rice: *"Palestinian State in 2008."* Praise God for thwarting this fallacy—another American fallacy.

It seems Mubarak was afraid of America's betrayal of him, in light of the betrayal of the Shah of Iran in 1979, Saddam Hussein in 2003, and Israel with the question of settlements and defensible borders, something aggravated even more by President Mubarak Hussein Obama.

Pastor Carl Gallups, aka ppsimmons, produced a You

Tube: *Saudi Plant* which faithfully expresses what Rachel picked up on the Egyptian TV program, that Obama's plan included the destruction of Israel. And we see an escalation of tension and hatred of Israel by President Obama.

So the cat is out of the bag. After decades of subservient "Christian" US presidents, the Moslem/Oil/Mammon agenda finally decided to place a Moslem in the White House seeking the destruction of the Shi'ite leadership in Iran, the destruction of Israel, and the Islamization of the United States.

America is being invaded by millions of Moslem immigrants/refugees, many of them entering the US illegally on charter jet flights, paid for by the bribed gate-keepers.

The Jewish population of the US is about six million. I estimate that the Moslem population in the US today is about 30 million: 4 million Farrakhan Black Moslems, according to their own count; 7 million Sunni Arabs, according to the Arab Immigrant Association, and about 9 million Shi'ite Iranians who fled Iran after the fall of the Shah. We have not yet even taken into account, the Turks, Bosnians, Albanians, Indonesians, Indian Moslems, African Moslems, Somalis, and Chechens, etc.

The Jewish vote will soon be only a pale shadow compared to the Moslem votes in the US. God is preparing to shut down the Jewish Diaspora in the US, and Canada as well as Latin America and Europe.

In conclusion, America has changed over the last 100 years from being a Christian country to now being a mammon-oil country. My work over the last 26 years has been to try to restore the US to its Christian roots and traditions for the sake of the future of the US, Israel, and the entire human race. It is not oil and mammon that made America the greatest country on Earth, but God, the Bible and for the vast majority of Americans, Jesus Christ.

And I say this as a Jew of the Jews, with a lineage back to King David; who is not a Christian, but *does support* the Christian agenda in the US and the Western world. The bribery of oil and mammon are the causes for fallacious US foreign policy.

CHAPTER II

RUSSIA, UKRAINE, POLAND VS. TURKEY AND ISLAM

During a tourism visit to Moscow in June, 1994, I was interviewed on Radio Moscow's *"Radio Alef"* program in the Russian language. After studying Russian at NYU in New York City from 1966-68, and then at Hebrew University in Jerusalem from 1968-71, and being Sovietologist to boot, I was invited for a one-hour radio show in the Russian language at Radio Moscow.

To make sure the questions and answers were well-prepared, I worked for a few hours to write everything down in Russian and instead of speaking fluently in my inferior Russian, and in an impromptu manner, I basically read my answers out in Russian from my own handwriting after being grammatically checked.

The gist of my message was: "The US is no longer the enemy of Russia; neither is Europe; neither are the Jews or Israel. The enemy of Russia for over a thousand years has been Islam, and still is today."

My interviewer, Oleg Gribkov, told me that though the USSR had been disbanded, and there was no more Soviet Union, but only the Russian Federation, he and most of his other co-workers were still Communists and believed in the Communist ideology of the *"Solidarity of all nations."* This meant that the Russian people would continue to have their friendly relations with the Moslem nations in total disregard of the wars being waged against Christian Russia by the Moslems, including the Taliban and Al-Qaeda during the Russian "Viet Nam" known as Afghanistan. It also included the different campaigns in Chechnya—wars that have been continuing for hundreds of years.

My confrontational approach to Islam was not what Communism taught. My answer to him was: "Don't be ridiculous! Islam has been attacking the Russians, the Poles and the Ukrainians for a thousand years. Their approach is: *'Kill the Jews on Saturday and the Christians on Sunday.'*"

Gribkov answered me saying: *"You know what? You are right!!! Let me tell you a little story every Russian schoolchild knows."*

"At the end of the Battle of Stalingrad, when the Nazi armies decided to surrender, there was only one group that refused to surrender. We must remember that the Nazi alliance brought in soldiers from Germany, Austria, Italy, Hungary, Romania, Bulgaria, Spain and finally Moslem soldiers from Albania, Chechnya and the British Mandate of Palestine. These Moslem soldiers were in their own Moslem SS unit and refused to surrender. They were known for their ferocity as fighters. Instead of surrendering, they charged with their bayonets drawn and their daggers clenched in their teeth. The Red Army machine-gunners just mowed them down."

The purpose of my message in Russia was to try to get the Russians, the US, the Europeans and Israel all onto the same page to defeat the Islamic threat to Western Judeo-Christian civilization.

But from what it seems, I believe we see the following happening. The US and the West back the Sunnis, and Russia and China back the Shi'ites. The Russians use the Shi'ites as

46

a proxy in their war against the West and the West uses the Sunnis as proxies in their war against Russia and China.

At the same time, as I mentioned in Chapter I, the Sunnis use the West as their mercenaries and proxies in the 1400 year war against the Shi'ites, and the Shi'ites use the Russians and Chinese as proxies in their war against the Sunnis. Of course, this is an over-generalization, and I hope to clarify this throughout the rest of the book. Chapter III will deal with the Sunnis and the Shi'ites. Chapter IV will deal with the Saudi nuclear missile base at the Al-Solayil Oasis. Chapter V will deal with the "Perfect Storm" or the final battle over Mecca in Saudi Arabia. Chapter VI will deal with efforts by the Moslems to flood the West with Moslem refugees/immigrants who will kill the Jews and certain Christians when orders for Jihad are given, leading to a massive flight of Judeo-Christians to the land of Israel, the expansion of Israel's borders, the conquest of Israel's neighbors, including Mecca and Medina and finally the rebuilding of the Temple in Jerusalem at the orders of the One World Government.

But before we get into the subject of Russia/Ukraine/Poland/Turks (Chechens, Tatars and Circassians), I wanted to give some background information about Spain in 1492. There are direct parallels to the multi-front war taking place in Eastern Europe. Indeed, I never understood why my B.A. Major in college was Sovietology and my minor was in Spanish and Latin and American studies. But there are clear direct parallel histories and cultures confronting Islamic invasions of Spain and Russia and the threat to their respective civilizations. These invasions were repulsed, at least until now, by Christian armies.

As a young high school student in New York, I was taken with my class to see *"Man of La Mancha"* a Broadway Play based on the book of Miguel de Cervantes, Don Quixote de la Mancha. The Broadway play itself was a spoof on chivalry in Spain in the 1600's. Americans are not taught the real meaning of what Cervantes was trying to share. True, he was protesting against the corruption of Spanish aristocracy and forgetting Spain's "noble" roots, but the politically incorrect message in this story is conveniently overlooked. Cervantes was trying to remind the Spanish of the Crusades against the Moslems. This was politically incorrect even then!

Miguel de Cervantes lost his right arm in the Battle of Lepanto in 1571, between the Spanish Catholic fleet and the Turkish Moslem fleet. The Spanish fleet defeated the Turkish fleet and broke the back of Turkish sovereignty over the Mediterranean basin.

This battle is almost never mentioned in American schools because it was a Catholic victory over the Moslems. And yet 17 years later, the Protestant English and Dutch navies defeated the Spanish Armada, and this, yes, is taught in American schools because it was a victory of the Protestants over the Catholics. But the Catholic victory was a turning point in what was almost 1000 years of warfare between Christendom and Islam. The Spanish Armada saved Western Civilization from Islam!

Whoever controlled the sea controlled the ground battles, just as today, whoever controls the air controls the outcome of almost any battle.

We mustn't forget that in 1492, Catholic King Ferdinand and Queen Isabella defeated the Moslems in Granada, and then expelled the Jews and Moslems from Spain; something considered at the time as a Holocaust by the Jews and Moslems, but they, the Christians, did it because in 1492, Spain was facing a fourth Moslem invasion; this time by the Turks. The Moorish kingdom of Boabdil in Granada was a threat to Christian Spain for possibly being a back door through which the Turkish fleet and armies could reinvade Spain.

The Turks in 1492 controlled the entire Mediterranean basin which included not only all of North Africa, but also the former Yugoslavia, Greece, Bulgaria, Romania, Hungary, and were at the gates of Vienna.

The Christian island of Malta withstood a massive attack by the Turkish fleet but remained victorious. In 868 the Arabs threatened to sack Rome if the Pope did not come up with a hefty ransom. For centuries, Sicily and the south of Italy were under Islamic rule.

Islamic marauders foraged into Poland, Ukraine and Russia as well. The Russian Orthodox Church was founded in 995 AD/CE by Cyril and Methodius partially as the answer to the Moslem marauders which could only happen if these Russian Slavic tribes became united. The Catholic Church was preeminent in Poland, and the Russian Orthodox Church being the same in Russia. And today, Western Ukraine is mostly Catholic and Eastern Ukraine mostly Orthodox.

In Yugoslavia, a microcosm of the struggles taking place more to the north and east, the Croats were Catholic. The Serbs were Eastern Orthodox. The Bosnians were Bogomils, a heretical Christian sect which later became Moslem, under the Turks, to receive protection from the persecution of the Croatian Catholics and Serbian Orthodox.

All three groups were from related Slavic tribes and they all basically spoke the same language.

To the south were the Albanians, a group whose language is totally unrelated to the Slavic languages or any other for that matter. The Albanians resisted the Turks under Skender Bey, but were finally subdued by the Turks and most became Moslems though a large minority remained Orthodox Christians.

We shall return to the realities on the ground in the Balkans a little further on in this chapter.

But it is important to stress the religious groups fighting both Islam and each other!

The Turkish armies were at the gates of Vienna. The Austrian royalty in the 1600's who were Catholic were now intermarried with the Spanish royalty which was also Catholic. So clearly, the Spanish were military allies of Austria. The Battle of Lepanto in 1571 helped to debilitate the Turks. It was the beginning of the end of the Turkish Empire.

Poland was another Catholic power. So they, too, were called to battle to save Vienna together with German barons.

In 2004, I had the opportunity to visit Poland. It was quite an unusual trip because the Polish group had very little money to pay me. They couldn't even pay a round-trip air ticket. They could, however pay for a train from Vienna to Warsaw and a one-way air ticket home to Israel.

So I called my dear friends in Basle, Switzerland, flew one way to my friends there, gave a lecture, and the next day, my Swiss friends drove me in their van to Bad Ischl in Austria near Salzburg, a 6-hour drive, where I spoke in a small Baptist church. The next day, my Austrian hosts drove me to the central train station in Vienna, and I took the "Jan Sobieski" train to Warsaw, Poland, an eight hour ride. After my lectures in Poland, I then took my one-way ticket back to Israel!

I had never heard of King Jan Sobieski until I took the train! Jan Sobieski, the Polish king in 1683 brought his army down to Warsaw and together with German barons, defeated the Turkish army's encirclement of Vienna, and again, broke the back of the Turkish army signaling another decline in Ottoman power in Europe. This was a cataclysm for the Turks just as the Battle of Lepanto a hundred years before.

This was a multi-front war and multi-century war. It

was also a multi-cultural war because the Turks were then pushed out of Hungary, Romania and Bulgaria and Greece and Yugoslavia. By 1912, the Turks were left with a sliver of land in Europe just across the Bosporus. That was it.

We must not forget the split between the Roman Catholic Church and Eastern Orthodox Church in 1053. This is a schism which, I think it is fair to say, has not been healed. There is still a lot of animosity between the Catholics and Eastern Orthodox. Another important date to remember is the fall of Constantinople and termination of the Byzantine Empire in 1453. The Catholic West did not come to the aid of Constantinople because of this animosity, and it fell to the Ottoman Turkish Empire! Constantinople which considered itself the replacement of Rome when it fell to the Huns was now replaced by Moscow as leader of the Orthodox Christian world.

An interesting anecdote: In one of my articles to the *Israel Today Magazine*, I wrote about the role of Poland and Jan Sobieski in routing the Turks who were besieging Vienna. I received a very interesting email from a Romanian who criticized me for praising the Poles and ignoring the Romanians. He said to me: *"We Romanians* (Orthodox Christians) *were fighting non-stop against the Turks for centuries until we defeated them. The Poles* (Catholics) *only fought one battle in Vienna!"*

The true importance of Count Dracula was in his bloody battles to defeat the Turks and free Romania from the Turks. He was not a blood-sucking vampire—which is what Hollywood turned him into.

American schools teach that Christopher Columbus was an adventurer who believed the world was round and that he could find an alternate route to the East Indies and the riches of Asia, which the Europeans were so fond of; riches like spaghetti, spices and gunpowder, a true capitalism success story!

But what the US and Western schools don't teach is that with the fall of Constantinople, the Silk Road to the East was now closed to the West and Moslems were trying to choke and starve Europe into submission to Islam. Christendom was surrounded and outnumbered.

What is not taught in US schools is that this was a defensive Christian religious war against Islam. The Crusades were a natural *response* to the Islamic invasions of Europe, the purpose of which was the termination of Christianity and Western Civilization. Colonization of Africa by the Europeans was a *response* to the Berber-North African slave trade and acts of piracy against the Europeans.

Columbus brought a great victory to the West. The gold and silver of Mexico and Peru helped to pay for the Spanish Armada which then went to defeat the Turks at Lepanto in 1571. Of course, much wealth was squandered on wars between the European Christian nations themselves!

European colonization of the Americas and Australia helped the Christian populations of Europe to break out of the Islamic stranglehold. This, in my opinion, was the greatest achievement of Christopher Columbus. Christendom was now no longer just Europe. It was now Europe, North America, South America, Australia, New Zealand and the Philippines. While the Christians grew in numbers and wealth, Islam became degenerate and in decline.

So 1492 was a great year for the expansion of Western Civilization, but it was also a horrible year for the Jews and the Moslems who were expelled from Spain.

It is also remarkable that the Jews who refused to convert to Catholicism were forced to leave Spain and Portugal and many went to Morocco or Ottoman Turkey which then included Yugoslavia, Greece, and Bulgaria. Many Jews became active in the Sultan's government and governance and some Jews were even active in the Turkish military with the keys to their homes in Spain still tied around their necks (hoping one day to return to their homes in Spain with the Moslem victory over the Christians.) Many believe that the influx of Jewish population into the Ottoman Empire in 1492 increased much of Turkey's greatness for a time. The Christian loss of its Jews became the gain of the Moslems.

Another area where the Jews moved to was the Black Sea area, then totally under Islamic-Turkish control. The Moslem Turks at that time saw the Jews as a welcomed asset for their empire, just as they were for King Boabdil in Granada until 1492.

Parts of what is today the Ukraine were basically under Turkish rule, so the Jews prospered under the Turks, while the Christians viewed them as enemies allied with the Turks.

So the Jews had two strikes against them: 1. They lived in the lands of the enemy Turks. And 2: The Jews were known to be agents of the King of Poland and collected taxes from the Ukrainians for the Polish King. For both these reasons, the Jews were hated by the Ukrainians and massacred by them.

In 1648, the "George Washington" of the Ukrainian national movement, Cmielnitzky, carried out a revolt against the Polish king and killed about half a million Jews, which, out of a total Jewish world population of 1 1/2 million Jews took the same toll on the Jewish people as did the Nazi Holocaust in WWII. The Ukrainians wiped out 1/3 of the Jewish nation.

This was the beginning of a very infamous and bloody relationship between the Jews and the Ukrainians.

At the same time that the Ukrainians were fighting the Polish King, the Russians were on the ascent and eventually subdued both the Poles and the Ukrainians (who were both

Catholic) and brought them under submission to the Czar of Russia who was Russian Orthodox.

So the different Christian churches were fighting each other in the East as the Protestant Reformation was now in conflict with the Catholic Church in the West.

And at the same time, Russians were now the vanguard in the war against the Turks. The Czarist armies moved southward and eastward into a "manifest destiny" parallel to the American manifest destiny. The Americans moved westward to the Pacific, and the Russians moved eastward to the Pacific.

About two hundred years ago, the German philosopher, Heinrich Heine, saw this happening and said: *"The world will have to choose between the foolishness of the Americans and the despotism and tyranny of the Russians."*

And indeed, Russia and the US have become chief competitors for global rule.

Just as the Americans subdued the Native Americans (Indians) or in Canadian terms, "First Nations", so too did the Czarist Russians subdue the different Turkish nations: Tatars, Chechens, and Circassians as well as other Islamic groups on the Russian march eastward, including the Mongols, Koreans, Chinese, and Japanese. Lermontov's book: *"A Hero for Our Times"* provides a narrative for a Russian officer in the newly conquered Islamic lands in the Caucasus.

I will never forget listening to an interview on Israeli radio with an officer in the IDF who was of Circassian extraction. He told a brief story about the Circassians in Israel and in Russia.

This interview took place during the Winter Olympics in Sochi, Russia in January 2014. This young Moslem IDF officer spoke about "Red Hill" in Sochi. He said that Sochi, considered today a "pure" Russian city was in 1854 a Circassian City, and that Red Hill was not red because of Communism but because of the blood of three million Circassians, whom he claimed were murdered by the Czarist Russians, a Russian version of a Holocaust of the Moslem Circassians.

Perhaps the Czarist slaughter of 1854 was part of the Crimean War of 1853-56 between Russia on the one hand and the British, French and Turks on the other. Here, again, the Western powers "gang up" on Russia. We must also remember that the British and French wanted Lesseps to build the Suez Canal in Egypt, which at that time was under Turkish-Ottoman rule, thus the British-French alliance with the Turks.

As a result of this ethnic cleansing by the Russians, most Circassian survivors then fled to Ottoman Turkey and then the Sultan sent many of these survivors to the Province of South Syria which was Israel of that time and these Circassians were posted as professional soldiers in the Turkish military garrisons.

When Israel received its independence in 1948, the Circassians, who were professional soldiers, remained loyal to Israel and to this day continue to serve as soldiers in the IDF. It must be remembered, that for all the criticisms of Israel around the world, the Israel Defense Forces have many Moslem soldiers including Circassians, Bedouin and others. The IDF also has other soldiers from minorities such as Christian and Druze soldiers. All of these serve Israel faithfully, and put to the lie that Israel is an apartheid state.

Although, I myself, certainly recognize the 1914-15 Armenian Holocaust, during which half a million Armenians were killed by the Turks, it may be that the Turks were taking revenge on the Christians by killing Armenian (pro-Russian) Christians just as the Russians killed Circassian Turkic Moslems in 1854. I don't justify either of the genocides.

At the end of WWI, Russia had lost much land to the Germans, who in turn were defeated by the allies: Britain, France and the US, and the new borders were drawn to allow for the rebirth of an independent Poland in 1920.

My grandfather, of blessed memory, served as a sergeant in this Polish army led by Josef Pilsudski, and fought the Soviets who were trying to re-conquer Poland and return it to Russian Soviet control.

At this point, I would like to relate a story about my grandfather's childhood in Warsaw, Poland. In 1914, my grandfather was 16 years old. The German army came into Warsaw and was seen as the liberators. The enemy of the Jews was the barbaric Russian Czar and his anti-Semitic government.

Pobedonovstev was the Russian Interior Minister, and had a policy toward the Jews: *"You kill a third, expel a third and convert the remaining third to Orthodox Christianity."* So my family, in Warsaw, Poland, then under Russian control was starving.

The German army came into Poland as the liberators of the Jews. They fed us, clothed us, and gave us work and income. They were our saviors. My grandfather went to work for the German army and supported his whole family from his salary.

The Germans taught my grandfather about copper wiring and demolitions. In the Polish war for independence and in the defense of Poland from the Soviets under Trotsky, my grandfather was in the engineer corps and used his demolition skills in the defense of Poland.

After the war, he emigrated to Argentina and opened a copper wire factory in Buenos Aires with the knowledge he acquired from the German army that was only kind to the Jews at that time.

It is here I wanted to mention my dear friend and colleague in the radio world, Michael Medved, who has interviewed me many times during my 26 years traveling to the US and Canada to speak in churches, synagogues, radio and TV.

After I told him about my grandfather in Warsaw, he told me about his grandfather: *"My grandfather on my mother's side was an officer in Kaiser's army (German army) and was deployed in Warsaw in WWI and was liaison to the Jewish community."*

This almost brought tears to my eyes. For it had to have been that his grandfather certainly knew my grandfather and took care of him!

He went on to say that Kaiser Wilhelm was the only leader in WWI to give kosher food to his Jewish soldiers and that Jews were disproportionately awarded the Iron Cross for valor in battle for Germany.

Many people cannot understand how the Jews just went sheepishly to their deaths in the concentration camps in Poland in WWII. But the truth is that the sign on the gate of the concentration camps: *"Arbeit Macht Frei"* (Work Makes you Free) brought back kind memories of the Germans in WWI. It was part of the Nazi deception to lure the Jews into the gas chambers without a fight.

Jews had not internalized what had happened in Germany with the rise of Nazism in Germany in 1933, and for them the German soldiers of WWII were no different than those in WWI. How deathly wrong they were.

The point I am trying to make here is that the Moslems in Spain and Turkey were our allies at that time in history, and today the fundamentalist Moslem agenda is the enemy seeking the annihilation or conversion of the Jews and Christians.

The Germans were our friends in WWI but killed six million of our people in the Holocaust in WWII. We Jews did not see it coming for the most part. Thanks to the Allied victory in 1945, Nazism was banned and the Germans for the most part returned to being a cultured, civilized and allied nation to Israel. The problem is not the people, the human flesh, but the satanic spirit that perverts good human beings and turns them into devils. Today, for the most part, the Germans are the "good guys" again.

The Russians were the enemy of the Jews in Poland in WWI, then in WWII, the Jews fought valiantly in the Russian army against the Nazis, the common enemy of the Jews and Russians which then became an ally.

Initially, Stalin recognized the nascent State of Israel in 1948 and then turned on the Jews with a Holocaust of his own, in 1953. But God thwarted Stalin's Holocaust plans for the Jews with Stalin's death on Purim 1953. How fitting! When Josef Stalin recognized the newly nascent State of Israel in 1948, he expected Israel to join the Soviet Bloc in light of the preeminent red flags flying throughout Israel representing both Communist and Socialist parties in Israel which dominated Israeli politics then. When Israel's first prime minister decided not to join the Soviet Bloc, and instead declared Israel's neutrality in the Cold War, Stalin became furious. But Ben-Gurion, to his credit, wanted to keep the doors open to the Jews of the West and the Western powers.

Today Russia has been a friend of Israel since the fall of Communism in 1989, and the re-establishment of diplomatic relations with Israel, severed during the Six Day War in 1967. We hope this continues, but it all could change depending on who the leader of Russia is, and what happens with the Iranian nuclear program or the Shi'ite/Sunni confrontation between Saudi Arabia and Iran. We also must not ignore what is happening in the Far East between China and its neighbors, especially over the Spratly Islands between Viet

Nam and the Philippines.

Ukraine was an enemy for centuries, but my own distant cousin who was shot three times by the Nazis in Babi Yar but not killed succeeded in returning to her apartment in Kiev and then was protected by her Ukrainian neighbors till the end of WWII. And the Ukraine has relatively good relations with Israel since it attained its independence from Russia in 1991. So there are good Russians and good Ukrainians after all!

Today, after more than a year of civil war with pro-Russian separatists, Israel is careful to draw a careful line between supporting the Russians or the Ukrainians.

But getting back to WWI, the Ukrainian nationalist leader Semyon Petlura, killed 100,000 Jews in his efforts to destroy any possible support for the Red Army as it retook the Ukraine and incorporated Ukraine in the Union of Soviet Socialist Republics (USSR). The Communist Russians then killed millions of Ukrainians through military executions and famine during the collectivization of Ukrainian farms in the 1920's and 1930's.

As a result of this mini-Holocaust by Petlura, Zeev Vladimir Jabotinsky, the mentor of Zionist Revisionists and today's Likud and other nationalist parties, told the Jewish world: *"Liquidate the Diaspora, or the Diaspora will liquidate you!"*

But the Jews of Europe wanted to hear nothing of Jabotinsky's plans to uproot themselves and leave Europe for the swamps and deserts of the British Mandate of Palestine.

Another testimony from another Michael, Michael Savage, must be mentioned here. On one of his radio shows, he said: *"Anyone who denies the Holocaust is guilty of two sins: Denying the Jewish Holocaust and denying the Christian Holocaust. In addition to the deaths of six million Jews, seven million Christians were also killed in*

59

the concentration camps."

We are also talking about the history of the Russians and the various Moslem tribes/nations in Crimea. Russia moves eastward from the European part of Russia all the way to the Pacific Ocean.

But this starts with the suppression of the Ukrainians and Poles, and then further south toward what is southern Ukraine and to the shores of the Black Sea. But in the 1800's, the north shore of the Black Sea was part of the Ottoman Empire, actually considered a Turkish lake.

The Tatars lived primarily in what is today Crimea. The Circassians were centered more to the east in what is today Sochi. And the Chechens lived in the Caucasus Mountains even more to the East.

In WWII, the Tatars sided primarily with Nazis. The Turks and Iranians, ethnically similar to the Tatars, admired Germany both in WWI and WWII, and this presented a threat to Soviet Russia.

So after WWII, Stalin expelled the Tatars, after the Nazi takeover of Crimea, and relocated them to an area called "Tatarstan." Ironically, the Tatars found oil and are collectively among the richest ethnic group in Russia today. Tatars expelled northward into the heart of Russia into something parallel to American Indian reservations—then left Tatarstan and returned to Crimea—400,000 of them.

Here is an interesting article from Yahoo/Reuters by Natalia Zinets dated March 22, 2015: KIEV (Reuters) - Turkish President Tayyip Erdogan offered a $50 million loan to Ukraine and called for the rights of Crimean Tatars to be protected during a trip to Kiev on Friday, but avoided outright criticism of trade partner Russia.

In a joint press conference with Ukrainian President Petro Poroshenko, Erdogan said Turkey was also offering $10 million in humanitarian assistance on top of the loan, which is meant to help Ukraine cover its budget deficit.

"We have expressed our support for the territorial integrity, political union and sovereignty of Ukraine, including Crimea, in every platform," Erdogan said, voicing support for the Minsk ceasefire brokered by Germany and France in February.

"We also wish for the continuation of Ukraine's stance of protecting the rights of all ethnic and religious minorities, especially Crimean Tatar Turks, who have proved their loyalty to their country during this crisis," he said.

Turks have close kinship bonds with the Muslim, Turkic-speaking Tatar minority in Crimea, the Black Sea peninsula Moscow annexed from Ukraine a year ago. Erdogan has repeatedly warned that the instability could have regional repercussions.

But Turkey has deepening trade ties with Russia and has been reluctant to openly criticize Moscow's actions in Ukraine. Erdogan spoke by phone with Russian President Vladimir Putin this week, discussing energy deals and the Ukraine crisis.

Russian gas exporter Gazprom said in January it planned to build an undersea gas pipeline via the Turkish-Greek border — a project informally known as "Turkish Stream" — as it seeks to supply Europe while by-passing Ukraine.

Ukrainian officials had been expected to seek assurances from

Erdogan and Energy Minister Taner Yildiz during their trip that those ties will not harm Ukrainian interests.

Asked at the press conference about the Turkish Stream project, Erdogan gave no new details, saying simply that Turkey found the Russian proposal "reasonable" and that Russia remained its biggest natural gas supplier.

A senior Turkish official said ahead of the visit that Ukraine's ambition to build a liquefied natural gas (LNG) plant on the Black Sea coast would be on the agenda, but that Ankara still opposes the project on environmental grounds.

"Nobody should expect from this visit a step from Turkey that could strain ties with Russia," a second official said ahead of the meetings with Poroshenko.

Just as Jews have felt a need to leave their host countries and return to Israel, so, too, did the Tatars desire to return to their original homeland in Crimea.

This is the second Turkic group.

The third group is the Chechens – the ethnic group of the Boston Marathon bombers who hated both Christian Russia and Christian America.

They fought the Russians for hundreds of years.

This is deeply embedded both in the Russian psyche as well as the psyche of these various Turkic groups. The Russians feel they are superior to the Moslem Turkic peoples.

At this point, it is also critical to understand the founding of Socialism, Communism, Bolshevism in the 1800's in which the former Jews, Christians and Moslems played a major role.

In *Fiddler on the Roof*, Tevye calls out to God: *"You chose us to be the Chosen People. Why can't you choose someone else? All we get from being so chosen is persecution and suffering."*

There was another type of Jew that did not want to be Jewish but sought a Godless system that would stop anti-Semitism or animosity of any kind between the different religions—Jewish, Christian or Moslem. Instead of the "New Man in Christ" in Christianity, we now had the "New man in Marx" in Communism and Socialism.

At the same time, we find reformers in the Islamic world: Kemal Ataturk of Turkey and the Shah in Iran; both suppressed Islam in order to modernize and westernize their countries or bring them out of the backwardness of Islam. So, too, there were Jews and Christians who became atheists, did not believe in God, and thought that God was at the root of all evil and suffering.

So the persecution of the Tatars, Circassians, and Chechens was of a national-religious nature until 1917. After 1917, the persecution was more of a left-wing, atheist system; call it Socialism, Communism, or Bolshevism, came against these Moslem nations and did everything they could to suppress Islam and Turkic nationalisms.

An important point to be stressed was that in 1917, the Russians under the Communists basically surrendered to the German armies of Kaiser Wilhelm II and lost tremendous amounts of territory to what later became independent Poland, Ukraine, Azerbaijan, Georgia, and Armenia.

After peace was attained with the Germans, the Russians, now Soviets, plotted to restore these lost lands to Mother Russia. And this is really what we see again happening today, after the disbanding of the Soviet Union in 1989.

Just as these Bolsheviks in Russia suppressed the

Poles, Ukrainians, and other Christian nations, so, too, they suppressed the Turkic ethnic groups.

Since the Ukrainians slaughtered the Jews in the hundreds of thousands in 1648, and during this civil war in Russia after 1917 until 1923, which later became the Soviet Union, so many of the Communists who suppressed Catholic nationalist, anti-Semitic Ukraine, were certain to take out vengeance on the Ukrainian people, and many of those avenging Communists were Jews with a collective memory for what the Ukrainians did to the Jews and would do so again if they could.

The Communist collectivization of the Ukraine and Russia brought about the deaths and executions of tens of millions of Ukrainians and Russians.

This was not forgotten by the Ukrainians, as well as the Turkic nations subdued by the Czars in the 1800's. So when the Nazis attacked Russia in June 1940, there was a tendency by the Ukrainians, Tatars, Chechens and Circassians to side with the Nazis against the Russians who had killed millions of these nations. It was kind of a "settling of accounts."

Even Romania, at that time an ally of Nazi Germany was given a piece of Ukrainian land known today as Moldova or Transdnistria – which had been part of the Ukraine, as a gift. The Russians want back Transdnistria, a Russian-speaking area and this could happen if Russia retakes Eastern Ukraine and continues its march westward into Transdnistria along the northern shores of the Black Sea turning what's left of the Ukraine into a landlocked country.

There was even an instance in which millions of Red Army soldiers were taken prisoner by the Nazis and offered to change uniforms as part of the Vlasov Army and return to the Soviet Union fighting the Soviets! (Vlasov was a Russian general taken prisoner by the Nazis who was convinced by

64

the German general staff to change sides and lead this now anti-Soviet Russian military force. Indeed many indigenous Russians hated Stalin and Communism.)

And of course, many Palestinian Moslems flocked to join the Nazi armies and even fought in a special SS unit exclusively comprised of Moslems soldiers. I referred to this earlier in this chapter.

So there were indeed a lot of unhappy people trapped in the USSR who supported the Nazis. The Jews entirely identified with the Soviet-Communist system and fought valiantly against the Nazis, Ukrainians, and pro-Nazi Turkic groups in enforcing the new atheist Communist system.

Some estimates put the deaths under Lenin, Stalin and the Soviet collectivization of the farmlands at between 30 and 40 million people.

After the re-conquest of Ukraine and the defeat of the Nazis, there was also considerable revenge taken out by Stalin's forces against those suspected of being collaborators with the Nazis: Ukrainians, Tatars, and other Moslems, as well as the pro-Nazis groups in the Baltic States: Latvia, Lithuania and Estonia.

After the death of Stalin, his successor, Khrushchev, a Communist but also an ethnic Ukrainian, decided in 1954 that the time had come to placate the Ukrainian people for all the suffering they had undergone under Soviet Communism. This became known as "Khrushchev's folly."

He did this by doubling the size of the Ukraine by giving the Ukraine lands to the east of the Dnieper River. As long as the Ukraine remained part of the Soviet Union, it didn't really matter if Russia ceded some land to the Ukraine, but in 1989, with the breakup of the Soviet Union, all of a sudden, Ukraine breaks away to establish an independent country taking with it Russian industries, lands, military bases, and population.

The Ukrainians then imposed laws on the Russian-speaking population in the eastern Ukraine banning the Russian language and forcing these ethnic Russians to speak only Ukrainian, a related but still different language.

At the same time, Ukraine wanted to join NATO and the European Union, something that meant, for the first time in history, they would then be breaking away from Russian hegemony and domination turning to the West. The Russians see Ukraine as its backyard and more importantly the origins of Russia. This could not be tolerated by the Russians.

We mustn't forget the poisoning of former Ukrainian President Yushenko by the Russians, and the victory of the Russian-backed candidate, Yanukovitch in the following elections. But Yanukovitch in typical eastern European tradition was extremely corrupt, palaces and all and finally, with the Ukrainian economy in horrible shape was removed from power after the big demonstrations in Maidan Square in Kiev in the spring of 2014.

The Ukrainians were insistent on turning westward and joining former Soviet-bloc countries Poland, Czech Republic, Slovakia and the Baltic States in joining the EU and NATO to provide their people with a better economy and living standard.

This brought about the rebellion of the eastern part of the Ukraine, the areas originally part of the Russian Soviet Socialist Republic, and ceded by Khrushchev to the Ukraine with a population of about ten million Russian ethnic people, the industries of eastern Ukraine and the naval bases in strategic Crimea.

Russian President Vladimir Putin was "reclaiming" Russian territory and working to re-integrate this land back into Mother Russia. I don't believe Putin is seeking to conquer all of the Ukraine, merely the Russian speaking areas to the east of the Dnieper River, the borders between Russia and Ukraine before 1954.

At this point, I want to change gears and give some background to what many call the "One World Government" with the European Union at its heart.

The Ukrainians chafed under Polish rule, and then under Russian and Soviet rule for hundreds of years. In order to fulfill their desire to distance themselves from Russia, Ukraine needs a patron to protect them from Russia to the east, and that's the European Union (EU) to the west. The Ukrainians are also seeking a better standard of living for their people – something easier to achieve with the West rather than the East.

It can even be said that many in Russia would also just love to join the EU to achieve better living standards for the Russian people. Many in Russia oppose Russian intervention in Ukraine leading to civil war between the Russian eastern provinces and the Catholic nationalist western provinces. Russian President Vladimir Putin, I believe, will be facing increasing opposition from within Russia by disgruntled citizens who oppose the economic downslide of Russia as a result of the Ukrainian intervention.

So I feel it is incumbent to give a little history here. Some might call it a conspiracy theory, but please bear with me as I develop this idea.

The Europeans have a history of many centuries of wars between different Christian, white, European nations fighting each other and slaughtering each other. Of course, we saw this between the Poles, Russians, and the Ukrainians. We also saw this in the Balkans between the Orthodox Serbs, Catholic Croats and Moslem Bosnians and Albanians.

During the Protestant Reformation, we also saw wars

between Protestant England and Holland vs. Catholic Spain. Napoleonic France fought against virtually all of Europe. Germans fought the French and the rest of Europe a number of times, and the list goes on.

I believe WWII was the "last straw". European leaders asked themselves the following question: "Are we crazy? Why are we white, Christian, Europeans killing each other?"

And so, after WWII, Belgium, Holland and Luxemburg decided to form Benelux, a customs union intended on simplifying commerce between these three little countries, and this then spread to include other nations becoming the "Common Market." Finally, the Common Market became the European Union (now) comprised of 31 nations. Customs barriers came down and a new common currency, the Euro replaced the currencies of many of these component countries.

European leaderships until WWII were by and large religious and nationalist and continued the traditions of centuries of wars which killed hundreds of millions of people over narrow religious and national considerations.

The European Union basically "abolished" war between these white European nations, and basically blamed religion and nationalism as the enemy of the Europeans and the entire human race.

Europe became "post-Christian" and "post-nationalist". Individual nationalisms became condemned and all member nations of the European Union had to basically suppress those instincts which were considered the causes of all these wars. And on the surface it worked. There have been no wars in white, Christian Europe since then.

There was a Balkan war over the disintegrating former Yugoslavia between Catholic Croats, Orthodox Serbs and Moslem Bosnians and Albanians. But wars between Christian states will not be tolerated any more.

And indeed two new Moslem countries were created out of the former Yugoslavia: Bosnia and Kosovo. And that is in addition to the Moslem Albania. Macedonia, which is 40% Islamic and 60% Christian population, will probably be next in line to become a Moslem country in Europe. The European Union invariably backs the spread of Islamic states on the European continent. Or at least, Europe will not oppose Islamic takeover of formerly Christian countries. So European equivalency of Christian nations in Europe now covers Christian-Moslem countries in Europe.

We saw how NATO heavily bombarded the Orthodox Serbs in order to bring the Serbs under submission in order to create Kosovo and Bosnia as Moslem states. The Serbian contention is that "Greater Serbia" has been broken up by the more Catholic European Union favoring both the Moslems but also the Catholic Croats and Slovenians. The Eastern Orthodox Serbs are identified with the Russians, whereas the Catholic countries are at the heart of the EU.

Serbia is backed by the other orthodox countries in Eastern Europe including Russia, Greece, Romania and Bulgaria. And the Ukraine is clearly seeking to come under the European umbrella of protection and "co-prosperity sphere" since it is also Catholic.

This rattles the Russians who fear attacks from the West on various fronts including Catholic Poland and Protestant or Catholic Baltic States: Latvia, Lithuania and Estonia. This has been the case for centuries going back to the wars with Scandinavian Norway/Sweden during the reign of Peter the Great, the Napoleonic wars and the German attacks of WWI and WWII.

But again, nationalism and religion in the European Union have been replaced with economics and the love of money, which is much more achievable with a "One World

Government" in Europe. Because after all, it's all about the money, right?!

Russia and the Orthodox countries are considered the "fly" in the ointment because they remain religious and nationalist by and large. That's why NATO ganged up on the Serbs during the breakup of Yugoslavia in the early 1990's.

But the world looks at Russia as the real "troublemaker". President Vladimir Putin has gone on record as saying that what made Russia great was its Christianity. Who could have believed such an outrageous statement by the former KGB agent? Russia under Communism was officially atheist and anti-religious and today Putin is considered a Christian and has declared: *"What made Russia great is its Christianity!"* So Russia is still guilty of the old-fashioned religion and nationalism.

Today, Russia is undergoing a remarkable religious and nationalist revival, while at the same time it seems Christianity is dying in the 31 nations of the European Union.

In the US, it's not much better. US Homeland Security quotes from its manual that the true terrorists are Christians, and Bible believers are mentally unstable. Sadly, America is no longer a Christian country according to the present agenda.

Therefore, the European post-Christian system sees Russia as an enemy that refuses to buckle under to the anti-Christian, anti-nationalist system of the European Union.

Below is a short article taken from Yahoo News on Monday, March 23, 2015 about nationalist/religious supporters from Western countries coming to Moscow to lend support to Russia and to Vladimir Putin:

European far-right politicians in Russia to support Putin ST. PETERSBURG, Russia (AP) — Nationalist supporters of Russian President Vladimir Putin brought together controversial far-

70

right politicians from across Europe on Sunday in an effort to demonstrate international support for Russia and weaken European Union commitment to sanctions imposed on Russia over its role in Ukraine.

Putin's critics pointed to the irony of St. Petersburg, his hometown, welcoming neo-Nazis as Russia prepares to celebrate the 70th anniversary of the Soviet Union's victory over Nazi Germany in World War II.

The meeting drew about 40 protesters, who held signs denouncing fascism, and about eight of them were detained by police.

Among the more prominent Europeans at the gathering was Nick Griffin, the expelled former leader of the anti-immigrant British National Party, who accused the U.S. of aggravating the confrontation in Ukraine, where more than 6,000 people have been killed in fighting between government troops and Russia-backed separatists.

"The people running the U.S. and their puppets in the European Union are doing everything they can, whether deliberately or just by stupidity, to drag us into a terrible war," Griffin said.

He spoke out against the EU sanctions, as did Udo Voigt, a senior figure in Germany's neo-Nazi fringe National Democratic Party, who was among several members of the European Parliament who attended the St. Petersburg gathering. Griffin lost his seat in the EU body last year.

71

Roberto Fiore, leader of Italy's far-right party Forza Nuova, and members of the neo-Nazi Greek party Golden Dawn also were among the approximately 200 participants.

The Russian nationalists who participated included Alexei Zhuravlev, a member of Russia's parliament, and Cossacks. Many Cossacks, descendants of the czarist-era horsemen who defended Russia's borders, have fought alongside the separatists in eastern Ukraine.

The participants had planned to sign a resolution at the conclusion of the forum, but the hotel where they were meeting was evacuated because of a bomb threat and they dispersed.

So I believe we are seeing here a convergence of religious and nationalist Europeans coming together to oppose the post-Christian EU approach to gang up on Russia and anything Christian or nationalist, both ideologies seen as dangerous by the EU and Obama's US. I even think that Israel falls into the same category of being religious and nationalist like the Russians and Eastern Orthodox Christians.

As a side-bar, I would like to say that as an Israeli who loves a Jewish religious and nationalist Israel as well as a Judeo-Christian and nationalist USA, I can see Israel is perceived as a threat to the post-Christian European Union's ideology, as well as to the anti-Christian positions of President Mubarak Hussein Obama.

It seems to me that since people do, after all, need religion, we will be seeing a coming together of different religious and secular ideologies into what some people call a One World Religion. According to this system, all people pray to the same God (I say Allah of Islam is Satan and clearly not the God of Abraham, Isaac and Jacob). In 2009, I even received a three year jail sentence (suspended) in Switzerland for saying that Allah is Satan and that Islam is a criminal psychosis. Jews, Christians, and Moslems will all find themselves praying *"to the same God"* under this One World Religion.

Probably, this system will be led by the Vatican because various popes have said *"We all pray to the same God."* The Vatican claims over 1.2 billion followers, the largest in size of all the Christian denominations. The Vatican is also actively trying to bring back as many Protestant denominations under its tutelage as possible, with varying amounts of success.

At this point, I wanted to give some of my insights into the Vatican. In spite of my preference for the Protestants, or at least some of them, who have definitely blessed the Jews more than the Catholics, in the overall Christian world, I have had occasion to befriend certain Catholics who have also been generous in assisting me on forming the Judeo-Christian Bible Bloc Party.

About thirty years ago, I met a rabbi from Iran who told me that the Koran was written by a rabbi. This was corroborated orally by many more rabbis. An Armenian Christian friend told me that the Koran was written by a Christian (Syrian) Orthodox priest.

I incorporated this message into my overall message on Islam, and received a call from a dear Catholic friend in Wisconsin, who invited me to meet with him. He had read a book, *"The Life and Religion of Mohammed"* written by a Catholic Jesuit priest, Menezes in 1912, clearly stating that the Koran was written both by a Christian priest as well as by a Jewish rabbi.

This began a friendship which has lasted until today. I have traveled numerous times to Wisconsin to meet this gentleman and some of his friends, who also contributed to the creation of the Bible Bloc Party.

In January 2014, I was invited to the Vatican to meet with Fr. Norbert Hoffman, responsible for Catholic-Jewish relations in the Vatican. At the very last moment, my cardiologist insisted on my having a stent procedure exactly on that day, and so my son, Aaron, CEO of Lipkin Tours traveled in my place to meet with Fr. Hoffman, who wanted to get an impression of who I was, as well as my son, and what my party stood for.

Fr. Hoffman told my son that upon returning to Jerusalem, we should me with Vicar David Neuhaus, a former Jew who converted to Catholicism.

A few months later, Vicar David Neuhaus spoke at the Van Leer Institute in Jerusalem. So I went to listen to him. He spoke about current affairs in the Catholic Church in the Holy Land. It was an interesting lecture. But when the time came for questions and answers, I asked him what he thought about the creation of a Judeo-Christian Party to run for the Israeli Knesset elections.

Without flinching, he answered: *"If the intention of this Judeo-Christian party is to 'gang-up' on the Moslems, the Catholic Church opposes it."*

I gave him a copy of my fourth book: *"Israel's Bible Bloc."* He said he could not wish me success from what he understood, from the gist of nature of this Judeo-Christian Bible Bloc Party!

His reason for being pro-Moslem and pro-Palestinian is because most of the Catholic Church members in Israel are Arabic-speaking Palestinians and so the Catholic Church cannot go against the Moslems or Palestinians.

At this point, I wish to relate something that appears in my first book: *"Is Fanatic Islam a Global Threat?"*

In early January, 1991, an article appeared in Israel's English-language daily, *"The Jerusalem Post"* regarding an article written by Father George Abu-Khazen in the Franciscan Order's magazine *"Terra Sancta"* blaming Moslems (for the first time) for Christian depopulation/of/ across the Holy Land.

Father George Abu-Khazen received a fatwa or death sentence from the Hamas. In a plea-bargain the Franciscan order had all the November-December issues of 1990 removed from the book stores to placate the Hamas and avoid Father Abu-Khazen from being killed by Hamas.

With great difficulty and daring, I must say, I went to the Franciscan Orders headquarters in the Christian Quarter of the Old City of Jerusalem and got a copy of the Nov-Dec 1990 edition, which I still have in its original Italian language.

I immediately took this to the Israel Defense Forces Spokesman's Office where I served as a reserve officer and spokesman for translation from Italian into Hebrew, and then I retranslated the article into English for my book.

For the first time, a Catholic magazine article blamed the Moslems for the flight of Christians from the Holy Land. Bethlehem used to be 90% and is now 90% Moslem. Nazareth went from 90% Christian to 65% Moslem. It's not the fault of the Jews or Israel, but of Islam.

In fact, former Bethlehem Mayor, Elias Freij, met with former Israeli Prime Minister Yitzhak Rabin in 1991 and begged Rabin to annex Bethlehem to Israel and Jerusalem to protect the Christians of Bethlehem and the territories.

Rabin agreed on the condition that the Catholic and Greek Orthodox churches provide letters to the Israeli government supporting the Israeli annexation of Bethlehem but the response of these two churches was that they stood with the Palestinians much to the detriment of their own parishioners. The Catholic Church and the Greek Orthodox Church did a disservice to their own people. And that's the real reason for the depopulation of the Christians in the Holy Land, contrary to the rubbish being spread at the "Christ at the Checkpoint" movement.

So if the Catholic Church and Greek Church don't care about their own people, why should these two churches be "Zionist?"

In fact, there is a very courageous Greek Orthodox Priest, Gabriel Naddaf, who was excommunicated from the Greek Church for calling on all Arabic speaking Christian youths to serve in the Israel Defense Forces just as there are Druze, Moslem Arabs, and Circassians, serving in the IDF.

Father Naddaf told me that the Arab Spring, which began in February 2011, was proof that the Moslems were no friends of the Christians and are now engaging in genocide against the Christians of the Middle East. The Jews, he said, are the true and only friends of the Christians.

It took 2,000 years for these Christians to overcome a tradition of anti-Semitism and replacement theology.

I am hoping that the Arabic-speaking Christians with whom I am in contact will embrace my **Gush Hatanakhi Judeo-Christian Zionist Party.**

But we also find replacement theology in certain Protestant churches, such as Lutheran, Methodist, Presbyterian and the "Emergent Church" or "Purpose-Driven Church," which are clearly examples of churches virtually abandoning Bible teachings and ceasing to preach the Gospel, so as not to offend anyone.

One of the reasons to assume the suppression of nationalist-religious nations and governments is the overwhelming demographic numbers in both the European as well as American continent blocs as opposed to the smaller populations in Russia and Israel. Here I want to share some useful population statistics.

Europe today, in the 21st century, totals about 350 million people, including about 50 million Moslems. The European Union thus outnumbers the US with a population of about 310 million people. The greater the population the greater the GDP is going to be usually.

To counter this problem, NAFTA (North American Free Trade Agreement) seeks to increase the population of the North American nations: Canada, Mexico and USA to about 500 million people which would then make the North American population greater than the European Union combined population. It also helps to explain the relatively free and open borders for children and their parents from Central America entering the US as refugees. I believe Central America and perhaps Colombia in South America could join NAFTA to increase the human numbers in this bloc.

So the European Union then seeks to bring Turkey which has a territorial foothold just across the Bosporus and itself also wishes to join this "co-prosperity sphere" of the Europeans. Turkey's population totals about 70 million which would give the Europeans a combined population of 420 million. But in addition to the 70 million, there are about 200 million Turkic Moslems in the six former Soviet republics which broke away from Russian control in 1989: Kazakhstan, Uzbekistan, Kirghizistan, Turkmenistan, Tajikistan and Azerbaijan.

There is also a Turkic Moslem population in the western Chinese province of Sinkiang demanding independence from Beijing, something that the Chinese people will never agree to. All Turks or Turkic peoples are entitled to Turkish passport just as all Jews are entitled to automatic citizenship in Israel.

So theoretically, the potential population of Europe with the Turks and Turkic Moslems could reach over 600 million.

Now the NAFTA group is short 100 million people. The answer is to bring in Moslems – primarily Arabs from the Arab Spring nations that have collapsed after February 2011.

So we are looking at two primary blocs: The America Bloc with 600 million people, and the European Union with 600 million people.

Meanwhile, the Russians (formerly the Soviets) with a population totaling 350 million, have lost most of their Moslem populations, and are left with 150 million Russians after they lost the 200 million from the former Turkic republics of the USSR. (And still the Moslems that remain in Russia are reproducing in much greater quantities than the Jews and Christians of Russia, and soon, Moslem conscripts in the Russian army will reach parity with the Christians.)

Since GDP is usually related to population, the greater the population the greater the GDP, the wealth and the military power.

Ukraine contains 10 million ethnic Russians in the rebellious provinces which, if added to the 150 within the Russian Federation would bring it up to 160 million, still far short of the Americas and EU. There are a few more million Russians in the Baltic States as well as Transdnistria in what is formerly Moldova. But Russia's economy today is at about the same in GDP as Italy. Russia wants back its land, population, factories, and military bases.

One thing both the Americas and Europe have in common is that the prevalent Moslem populations in both, Arabs or Turks or others, are primarily Sunni Moslems. The Sunnis see the Russians as an enemy of 1000 years.

The Russians for their part have very friendly relations with the Shi'ite Moslems, enemies of the Sunni Moslems led by Iran.

Of course, the Russians in the past, were suppliers of weapons and support to Egypt, a Sunni country as well as Libya and Iraq during Saddam's rule. And today, Russia and Egypt, under President Abdul Fattah al-Sisi, have drawn closer together for a short time as President Obama has distanced himself from General and President al-Sisi who overthrew the Moslem Brotherhood and the former president Mursi.

Even as I write this book in mid-May, 2015, it seems the Obama Administration may be reconsidering its policy regarding Egypt and returning to its prior policy of arming Egypt as part of what seems to be shaping up as an anti-Russian, anti-Iran, anti-Shi'ite, anti-Chinese alliance.

What I feel is happening is that the America bloc and the European Union are supporting and being supported by the Sunnis, while the Russians, Chinese, North Koreans are closer to the Shi'ites, the sworn enemies of the Sunnis for 1,400 years.

At the same time, the Vatican in Rome is trying to unite the Catholics and Protestants under one umbrella by bringing the Protestant churches under the Vatican's sway. The Vatican is also clearly refusing to behave in a confrontational approach to the threat of Sunni Islam to Europe, Christianity and the World, as Christians are beheaded by the Sunni ISIL terrorists and churches are being destroyed in a Holocaust of the Christians by the Moslems in the Middle East. And meanwhile, Shi'ites, the supposed "enemy" are actually protecting their Christians in Syria, Iraq, and Lebanon.

So the One World Government in my opinion, includes the America bloc, the European Union, and the Vatican in alliance with the Sunnis.

The Russians, Chinese, and North Koreans support the Shi'ite bloc of Iran, Iraq, Bashar al Assad's Syria, Hizbullah in Lebanon, as well as the Shi'ite populations in the Persian Gulf, and most recently the Houthis in Yemen, all suffering from persecution, discrimination and disenfranchisement at the hands of the Sunni regimes in those countries, while the West uses the Sunnis as proxies in the war against Russia and Russia uses the Shi'ites as proxies against the West.

At the same time, the Sunnis use the West as their mercenaries against the Shi'ites and the Shi'ites use the Russians and Chinese as their defenders and proxies against the Sunnis. It would seem to me that the Shi'ite/Russian bloc is outnumbered by the Sunni/Western bloc.

CHAPTER III

SHI'ITES VS. SUNNIS

It is not the purpose of this book to provide a full and complete history, either of the Sunnis or Shi'ites in Islam, but simply to provide an up-to-date overview of the struggles between these two groups and their sponsors, and to show the inevitability of a final showdown in Mecca, the holy city of Islam.

But it is important to stress briefly the main reason for the split between the two and the resulting 1400 years of wars between them, with no hope for forgiveness, love, and reconciliation, and most important of all, an end to the strife between them.

Before he died, Mohammed reputedly had a dream that after his death, his camp of followers would split into two and that only one of the two groups would enter heaven. He didn't know which group was destined for Heaven and which was damned. He had no idea how prophetic that would be.

After his death, Mohammed's closest confidantes and followers replaced him consecutively as caliphs or replacements. The first was Abu Bakr, then Othman and then Omar. These men followed Mohammed into battle and were wounded alongside Mohammed. These are the fathers of the Sunni branch of Islam.

The fourth caliph was Mohammed's flesh and blood: Ali. Being an orphan, Mohammed was raised in the home of his

Uncle Abu Talib who was also the father of Ali. So Ali was Mohammed's first cousin but more like a little brother since they were both brought up together.

Indeed, Fatima, Mohammed's daughter married Ali, her first cousin, something considered an honor and tradition amongst Arabs although biologically a threat to the family's health because of the defects of genetic inbreeding.

Ali and Fatima then had children, with sons Hassan and Hussein being the most prominent of them. This was the beginning of the Shi'ite branch of Islam.

As the family grew and matured, a struggle for control began between the followers of the three first caliphs and the followers of Mohammed's children.

It must be remembered that under these four caliphs, tremendous amounts of territory, wealth and power were accumulated, and the question was of who exactly was going to rule and control this wealth and power. It was a turf battle, much like Mafia families, and like Mafia families, often resulted in bloody feuds and turf-wars.

When the feud reached its height, both of Mohammed's grandsons, Hassan and Hussein were beheaded by the Sunnis (followers of the first three caliphs) and their heads were prominently carried around the streets of Baghdad on poles to show what happens to those who support the dynastic family of the prophet.

This was the beginning of what was to become 1,400 years of persecution of the Shi'ites by the Sunnis.

Today, about 85% of Moslems are Sunnis and 15% Shi'ites. But the Shi'ites are mainly concentrated in the Persian Gulf countries reaching a 50-50 proportion to the Sunnis. This is the making for a perfect, never-ending, storm, culminating, I predict, in the final battle for Mecca in Saudi Arabia in which both sides lose and Islam is terminated by the One World Government that has simply had enough. I will elaborate at the end of this book.

There is a joke I always like to tell in churches, synagogues, radio and TV to show the difference between the rivalries of the Moslems vs. the rivalry of the Catholics and Protestants:

"This Catholic Priest, Father O'Malley was attacking the Protestants from his pulpit in Belfast, Northern Ireland.

"So he gets this telephone call from the archbishop speaking in an Irish accent: 'Father O'Malley, I have been receiving reports that you are bashing the Protestants in Northern Ireland. We are working for peace in Northern Ireland. Is that clear? From now on you will preach the Gospel at the High Mass.'

"So Father O'Malley got up on his pulpit at mass on Sunday morning and delivered his sermon: 'Jesus was having his last supper and told his disciples with his Irish accent: 'One of you will betray me.'

"One of his disciples, Matthew got up and asked: 'Is it I?'

"No, answered Jesus."

"The next disciple, Mark got up: 'Is it I?"

And so it was with eleven of the disciples.

"Finally, the twelfth disciple, Judas, gets up and asks with his British (Protestant) accent: 'I say old chap, is it I'?"

This is absolutely one of the best jokes in my inventory given to me by John Loeffler of Steel on Steel Ministries in Idaho.

But the point here is that after 300 horrible years of killing, torture and wars, the Wars of Reformation between the Catholics and Protestants are over.

As a Jew, I love both Protestants and Catholics. I also love Moslems. But you don't see Protestants and Catholics slaughtering each other anymore, praise God. Christians matured and learned to live together. But the Moslems, on the other hand, have been slaughtering each other for 1,400 years and there is no end in sight!

The UK, USA, Canada and Australia are examples of how Catholics and Protestants live together, live in peace, and there are even intra-marriages between them with families sometimes attending a Catholic church and the following week a Protestant church.

I saw this with my own eyes in towns where people came to hear me speak and I saw them both in the Catholic and Protestant churches in which I spoke.

There is movement between the two primary systems but you don't see anyone murdered for changing from one denomination to another.

But in Islam, the killing has been going on for over 1,400 years with no end in sight. There has been no "Protestant Reformation" in Islam yet, nor do I believe that it could be possible. Because the God of Islam, Allah al-Ilahi, the moon-god, sword-god, and war-god, is really another form of Satan looking to kill the Jews on Saturday, the Christians on Sunday, the Hindus, Buddhist, Blacks in Africa any day, and then the Shi'ites and Sunnis kill each other, all in the name of that Satan-Allah. So, in my opinion, Islam cannot have a reformation and will not. The only outcome of such a system is total self-destruction – because they kill each other.

When they pray "Allahu Akbar", the Moslems are NOT saying: *"God is great."* What they are saying is that their God, Allah, is GREATER—greater than the Judeo-Christian God of Abraham, Isaac, and Jacob. Wasn't it Satan who said he was greater than God before his expulsion from Heaven?

The God of Abraham, Isaac, and Jacob loves the Jews. In Zachariah 2:12, it says that the Jews are the apple of God's eye, and anyone who touches the Jews, touches the apple of God's eye. God also says in many places in the Bible that His covenant with the Jews is for 1000 generations, i.e. forever.

The God of Abraham, Isaac, and Jacob loves the Christians. In Romans 9-11, Christians are told they are *"grafted into the Jews."* The Jews are the roots and the Christians are the branches. Would God have grafted the Christians into the Jews if he hated either of them?

The God of Abraham, Isaac, and Jacob loves the pagans, the Hindus, the Buddhists, and the Blacks of Africa. Love the sinner. Hate the sin (of paganism) because all are his children.

And the God of Abraham, Isaac, and Jacob loves the Moslems, whose god is the Devil because we must love the sinner and hate the sin.

And all human beings were created in the Divine Image. We are all his children. But Satan cannot say he is "greater" until all those created in the image of God are dead.

Allah al-Ilahi/Satan hates the Jews and wants them dead on the Sabbath, because the Jews keep the Sabbath. Allah-Satan wants the Christians dead on Sunday, because Christians keep the Sunday. Allah-Satan hates the Hindus, Buddhists, and Blacks in Africa and wants them dead any day. And finally, the Shi'ites and Sunnis slaughter each other at any time in Allah-Satan's name until there are no more human beings left.

How can God and Allah be the same God? How can God love everyone and hate everyone at the same time? All humans were created in His image, and Allah hates all humans and wants every human being killed including the Shi'ites and Sunnis? Indeed Islam is the perfect system for destroying the entire human race. And that's why Islam must be, and will be, banned.

As I said previously, I received a three-year jail sentence (suspended) in abstentia in Switzerland for saying that Allah is Satan and that Islam is a criminal psychosis and not a religion.

In 2009, I was invited to deliver a total of 23 lectures in different cities in German-speaking Switzerland as part of the "Minaret Initiative" to prevent the Moslems from building minarets alongside the 400 mosques in Switzerland so that Moslems could declare their prayers from the loudspeakers five times daily.

It was the EDU right-wing and Christian religious party of Switzerland that hosted me. I told the Swiss that not only were the minarets going to spoil the quality of life of the Swiss people with the noise pollution of the loudspeakers at high decibels. I told the Swiss that the Moslems would be declaring their triumph and superiority over the Jews and Christians of Switzerland by proclaiming: Allahu Akbar or Allah is greater than the God of the Jews and Christians: the God of Abraham, Isaac, and Jacob.

Praise God, on November 29, 2009, the Swiss people voted by a majority of 57.5% against 42.5% not to allow for the disaster which was the minarets of Islam. I told them that Switzerland would fall under Islam if the minarets were built.

Praise God, I was allowed to serve Him in the defense of Switzerland and the superiority of Judeo-Christian Western Civilization and Democracy over Islamic-Satanic plans for the destruction of modern civilization.

I was taken to court in abstentia without my knowledge, while outside of Switzerland, and have not returned to Switzerland since. One of the jokes I told the Swiss people every night was the following:

"What is the difference between neurotic people and psychotic people? Neurotic people dream about castles in the air. Psychotic people live in castles in the air."

Adolf Hitler was psychotic for two reasons: He thought he could conquer the Earth. He thought he could kill all the

Jews. Now, can anyone conquer the Earth? The Persians, Greeks, Romans, and Mongols all thought they could. Hitler, Stalin and Napoleon thought they could. They were ALL psychotic, living in castles in the air. No one can conquer the Earth and anyone who thinks he can is crazy. Only the Lord has dominion over all the Earth!

Secondly, he thought he could kill all the Jews. Now, can anyone kill all the Jews? There are two types of people: Believers and non-Believers. If you are a Believer, you know that God says in Jeremiah 35:31 that there will always be Jews on Earth, except when the Moon, Sun and Stars cease shining. That means forever.

For those who do not believe in God, everyone knows the Jews are scattered throughout the world. Now if one cannot conquer the entire world (psychosis #1) then one cannot kill all the Jews (psychosis #2) because it is impossible to reach all the Jews.

So Hitler was psychotic.

What does Islam believe?

Islam believes it will conquer the Earth. Secondly, it will kill all the Jews on Saturday, because the Jews are the Saturday People; kill all the Christians on Sunday, because the Christians are the Sunday People; kill all the pagans, Hindus, Buddhists and Blacks in Africa any day and finally, after 1/6 of the human race kills 5/6 of the human race, the remaining 1/6 of the human race, the Moslems, will then go ahead and kill each other. Sunnis will kill Sunnis, Shi'ites kill Shi'ites and then Sunnis and Shi'ites will kill each other all in the name of Allah.

So if Allah wants everyone dead, and the God of Abraham, Isaac, and Jacob wants everyone to live, then Allah cannot be God, the God of creation but instead, is Satan, the god of destruction seeking to prove he is greater than God by killing

87

all those created in the image of God. Allah is Satan, and Islam is not a religion, but a criminal psychosis that must be banned. Love the Moslems. Hate and defeat Satan and his system: the criminal psychosis of Islam.

This joke fairly represents the insanity and criminal psychosis of Islam. It says in the Koran, the book of Islam in Chapter/Sura V: verse 33:

"Anyone who wages war on Allah, his prophet Mohammed, or spreads disorder in the land, we will kill, crucify, chop their hands and legs and banish from the land."

So, of course:

The Jews are waging war on Allah…. So they must be killed. The Christians are waging war on Allah … So they must be killed. The Hindus are waging war against Allah, so they must be killed. The Buddhists are waging war against Allah, so they must be killed. The Blacks in Africa are waging war against Allah, so they must be killed.

And of course, the Sunnis say that the Shi'ites are waging war against Allah so they must be killed. And of course, the Shi'ites say that the Sunnis are waging war against Allah, so they must be killed. Guess what? Nobody left! Satan wins, God-forbid! So Islam's defeat is *inherent* and *inevitable,* contrary to what the Moslems think.

The following is a heartbreaking story about what Sunnis do to Sunnis in Algeria to this day. It is from an Aljazeera report two decades ago.

My wife, Rachel, saw an interview on Aljazeera TV with a young Algerian Salafist terrorist apprehended by the Algerian military during the ongoing civil war in Algeria since 1992.

The story of Algeria is indeed a tragic story because today, there are virtually no more Jews or Christians after the French left Algeria in 1962. It was known at that time that anyone who remained behind would be slaughtered, so all Jews and Christians left Algeria for the motherland; France.

There are no Hindus or Buddhists in Algeria and not too many African Blacks except for transients trying to traverse Algeria and risk their lives on flimsy boats to cross the Mediterranean and to enter Europe illegally.

There are no Shi'ites in Algeria, only Sunni Moslems. Algeria's population is homogenous, exclusively Sunni Moslems with Berber origins.

As I mentioned earlier, France occupied and colonized France in the 1800's in order to make sure the piracy and slave trade ended. But by 1962, former French President Charles de Gaulle came to the conclusion that the FLN (Front de Liberation National) the terrorists or freedom fighters of Algeria could not be defeated, and this war of suppressing the Algerian freedom-fighters was bleeding the French far too much. This was also after the debacle of Dien Bien Phu in Indo-China (Viet Nam) in 1953.

The FLN leadership was trained in, and backed by, the USSR. For the Soviets, it was a major victory that the French capitulated and withdrew.

This Algerian leadership was Sunni Moslem, but considered secular and ready to work with the Soviets in order to achieve independence and French de-colonization.

It was this FLN leadership under Ben Bella, Boumedienne, and others, who brought freedom to Algeria from the French. But being Moslems, their system could not be democratic and from 1962-92, Algeria was ruled as a Soviet-backed military dictatorship.

With the collapse of Soviet Communism in 1989, now it was the Russian Federation that was disengaging from much of its Cold War confrontations with NATO and the West.

So elections were called in Algeria in 1992 and the

Salafist fanatic Moslems won these elections, and their plan was to establish a fanatic, Shariah law system, considered inimical to what the founding secular Moslem leadership believed in, which was a more secular, socialist, system. So the founding leadership annulled the election results, and the Salafist victory, declaring that Algeria would not be allowed to become another Iran.

The result of this decision by the former FLN leadership was a civil war between the secular Moslem leadership of Algeria and the fanatic Sunni Moslems who were now the majority.

It says in the Koran: Sura V: verse 33: "Anyone who makes war against Allah and his prophet Mohammed and spreads disorder in the land, we shall kill, crucify, chop off their arms and legs, and banish from the land."

Obviously, the FLN secular Moslems were now waging a war against the Salafists, and so the above quote was applicable to these "infidel heretics." Over 200,000 Algerians have died since 1992: Sunni Algerian Moslems killing Sunni Algerian Moslems.

I don't remember when exactly. Probably it must have been about 20 years ago before the writing of my first book: *"Is Fanatic Islam a Global Threat?"*

My wife called me one evening while I was on a lecture circuit in the United States. Evening in the US was around 4AM in Israel, and my wife was crying hysterically.

She had just seen an interview on *"Al-Jazeera"* TV with an Algerian Salafist terrorist who had been apprehended by the Algerian military for helping to wipe out a village of Algerian "infidels." These people were murdered because the men of the village, somewhere in the mountains outside of Algiers, all served in the Algerian army, and therefore were considered as infidels, or people who were *"waging*

90

war on Allah, his prophet, Mohammed, and spreading disorder on the Earth."

So the Salafist terrorists reconnoitered the village for a few days, and when they understood that the men all went to work at 06:30 in the morning, they decided one morning to close off the village after the men were gone and wipe out the village.

Firstly, the Salafists would knock on the doors of the villagers, which at this point were the women, elderly and children. They instructed the women to cook them a meal. After the terrorists ate their lunch, they popped halucinagenic pills, got on a high and raped all the women. After raping the women, they slit the throats of the women, then slit the throats of the elderly, and then slit the throats of the children.

And it wasn't over. Then the terrorists went to their pick-up trucks, took out electrical chainsaws and sawed off all the arms and legs of their victims so that when the males of the village, all employed by the infidel military came home, they would understand the punishment meted out to those who *"fought Allah, his prophet, Mohammed and spread disorder on the Earth."* And this took place 20 years before ISIL!

My wife, Rachel, poor thing, had to take sedatives for at least a week. And this is the nature of Rachel's media tracking work for the last 30 years at Kol Israel in Jerusalem.

So, here we have the example of Sunni Moslems killing Sunni Moslems. In Shi'ite countries, the Shi'ites kill the Shi'ites, and of course, the Sunnis and Shi'ites kill each other because the Shi'ites see the Sunnis as infidels and heretics, and vice versa.

So what should Christians, Jews, Hindus, Buddhists and Blacks in Africa expect from the "religion of peace?"

And because, as I covered earlier in this book, the Moslems gave gained such inordinate power as a result of their petroleum supplies, cash inversion into the world economy, and now their immigration numbers into the Western countries, everyone is afraid to confront them.

Political correctness, the discoveries of oil supplies in Islamic countries and subsequent money has caused Western, supposedly Christian leaders, to acquiesce to the evils of Islam and thus become accomplices to the different genocides and war crimes the world has been witnessing over the last 100 years.

On the one hand, Islam has the entire human race in a choke hold, because of its oil, cash and population spreading all over the Earth.

It is true that from the Battle of Vienna in 1683, Islam had been on the retreat virtually everywhere on Earth, but with the development of the motor engine and the need for petroleum, Islam's fortunes have been on the rise over the last 100 years.

Colonization by Europeans began to end, already starting right after WWI, and this accelerated through the UN after WWII, but as I mentioned earlier in this book, the Saudis, who received their independence from Turkey at the end of WWI discovered oil in the 1920's and began to play a critical role in the world's decision-making including the killing of six million Jews during WWII.

Just as the Jews were expendable due to Saudi and Islamic pressure, so, too were the Shi'ites living in the eastern part of Saudi Arabia, a country whose rulers were Sunnis. To this day, the Shi'ites feel disenfranchised in Arabia.

In Bahrain, for example, the population is 70% Shi'ite, yet the king and the royal family leadership are Sunnis. When there is an internecine struggle between the Shi'ite majority and Sunni minority leadership, the Saudis send in troops to reinforce Bahrain's king and his family.

Kuwait is more or less 50-50 Shi'ite-Sunni with again,

a Sunni King and leadership. This reality is repeated in the Emirates and other Gulf nations and down to Yemen, where the Shi'ite Houthis, persecuted by the Sunnis, have just overthrown the established Sunni regime in Sanaa, the capital of Yemen. And the Iranians back the Houthis. This is something that must be followed carefully. Look at the atlas-map. Sanaa is a day's drive from Mecca, the holy city of Islam. This is where the final clash, the *perfect storm*, the main subject of this book, will take place.

What I want to do now is to briefly review the history of Iran, Iraq, Syria, and Lebanon, also commonly known as the Shi'ite crescent.

Iran, the preeminent Shi'ite country, was known as Persia and has a 3,000 year history, much of which was very pro-Israel and pro-Jewish. When the Jews were carried off to exile in Babylonia for 70 years in 586 BCE, it was Cyrus, emperor of Persia, who defeated the Babylonians and helped to restore or return the Jews to Jerusalem and the Holy Land 70 years later. Cyrus is described in the Bible as "The Messiah" who saved the Jews from their horrible predicament of exile along the rivers of Babylon.

Cyrus even sent his soldiers to accompany and protect the Jews on their trek back to the Land. Cyrus also sent gold and other offerings for the Jews to rebuild the Temple on Mt. Moriah.

In the 4th century BCE the Jews faced a horrible enemy in the body of Haman, an Agagite-Amalekite cousin of the Jews who sought to wipe out every Jew in the Persian Empire which stretched from Africa to India.

King Ahasuerus also known as Artaxerxes III, was not anti-Jewish, but was easily swayed by Haman and later by his Jewish Queen Esther and Mordecai her uncle and restored the Jews to their prominent role in his kingdom. So the problem was not the Persians or Persia. The problem was an individual leader's hatred of the Jews, and he, Haman, himself was not a Persian.

In 614AD/CE, the Zoroastrian Persian army conquered the Holy Land and delivered the Jews in the Holy Land from the horrible anti-Semitic edicts of Sophronius, the Byzantine arch-bishop. There was even talk of building the Third Temple on Mt. Moriah, but in 638 AD/CE, the Persian protectors of the Jews in Israel were defeated by the Arab invaders under Omar al-Khattab.

The new Sophronious-Arab pact of 638 called for no more Jews in Jerusalem.

The Arabs then went swiftly to conquer what is today Iraq and Persia and brought Islam to these countries. Iran later became Shi'ite.

During the Cold War between the US and the Soviets, the Shah of Iran, Reza Pahlevi was also an ally of the US and Israel, so much so that the Iranian nuclear project was actually initiated by the Israelis and the Americans.

In 1979, because of stupidity and ignorance, then-President Jimmy Carter, together with his adviser, Zbigniew Brzhezhinski, brought down the Shah, the cornerstone of American policy in the Near East against Soviet power, and turned Iran into something much worse than the Shah's dictatorship. Iran now became a revolutionary Shi'ite Islamic country threatening the entire world with terrorism and an atomic project aimed at acquiring nuclear weapons.

Between 1980-88, Iran was attacked by Iraq of Saddam Hussein in what became a bloody nine-year war. The results of this war were inconclusive, other than the deaths of over a million Iranians and Iraqis.

Since 1982, Iran has been involved in spreading its brand of revolutionary Shi'ite Islam. Hezbollah is Iran's proxy in Lebanon and has come to dominate Lebanon, while defending the Shi'ite-Alawite regime of the Assad family in Syria. Of course, Israel is considered a foremost enemy alongside the Sunni Moslems.

In 1983, Hezbollah blew up in two different truck-bomb attacks, both the US embassy in Beirut, Lebanon as well as the US Marines barracks killing 243 US Marines.

In 1992, the Iranians blew up the Israeli Embassy in Buenos Aires, Argentina and in 1994 Iranian terrorists blew up the AMIA building also in Buenos Aires killing 85 people and injuring over 300, and in 2015, were behind the murder of Argentine Prosecutor Alberto Nisman.

The Iranians control a mini-state straddling the borders of Argentina, Brazil and Paraguay, called the Eastern Triangle, or Terror Triangle. All forms of contraband can be obtained including dynamite, weapons, drugs, and counterfeit dollars.

As of March, 2015, we are waiting to see the results of world negotiations with Iran regarding their Iranian nuclear project. The possibility of a war between Iran and Israel over the nuclear project is a distinct possibility if Iran continues to pursue a nuclear arsenal of weapons against Israel.

There is also the possibility of war by an Arab alliance against Iran over Iran's intervention in wars in Lebanon, Syria, Iraq and Yemen.

Lebanon, Syria and Iraq were all parts of the southern Ottoman Empire just as Israel (Palestine), Jordan and what is now Saudi Arabia were parts of the Ottoman Empire until its defeat by the British and French in 1918.

Saudi Arabia got its independence, followed by the Hashemite Kingdom of Jordan in 1922 (in Transjordan, on land promised to the Jews in the Balfour Declaration of 1917) to mollify the Hashemites a rival tribe of the House of Saud. And of course, the Palestine Mandate became Israel in 1948.

Another country that received a Hashemite King for a

very short time was Iraq, also under British colonial control for a few years.

Lebanon and Syria, considered one unit, was divided up by the French into a Christian country Lebanon, and a Moslem country, Syria. But it was a known secret that by 1945, Lebanon had lost its Christian majority.

The Syrians do not recognize the independence of Lebanon, but merely see Lebanon as an extension of Syria seized by the French and torn away from the Syrian motherland.

Lebanon has four primary ethnic groups: Christians (Catholic and Eastern Orthodox), Druze, Sunnis and Shi'ites. Today the Christians are about 28%, and the Shi'ites about 40%.

Lebanon today, especially its army, is dominated by Hezbollah Shi'ites who are actively participating in the civil war next door in Syria. Hezbollah is heavily aided by the Shi'ite regime in Iran. What I am going to say now is definitely not my personal opinion but something I heard from Lebanese friends: The Sunnis, Christians and Druze view the Lebanese Shi'ites as backward, thus the surprise at the Iranians mobilizing them into the dominant political and military factor in Lebanon after 1982.

In Syria, 80% of the population is Sunni, but the ruling coalition of Syria is led by Alawite Shi'ites, led by the Assad family, who represent 10% of Syria's population together with 10% of Syria who are Christians plus Druze and certain Sunnis who are also part of the Assad power elites in Syria. So the Assad family leads about 50% of the population including certain Sunnis, while the rebel Sunnis who are all Sunnis belong to the various rebel groups including Jabhat al-Nusra and ISIS: the makings for the perfect never-ending storm. Today half of the Syrian population is displaced as refugees, and to date, over 200,000 Syrians on both sides have died.

Shi'ite Iran has been backing the Alawite Shi'ites of

Syria alongside the Russians and Chinese. The Sunni rebels who have been slaughtering the Shi'ites, Christians, Druze, Kurds and Yazidis are backed by Turkey and other Sunni, Islamic countries led by Saudi Arabia.

With the rise of ISIL in Syria and Iraq, we see a constellation of Saudi-backed American-trained Sunnis who were the stalwarts of Saddam Hussein's government disgruntled over their being disenfranchised by the Shi'ite-led government in Baghdad just as they, the Sunnis, disenfranchised the Shi'ites under Saddam Hussein.

The question as to, can there ever be reconciliation in Iraq, is an easy question to answer. Saddam Hussein, the Sunni, represented 20% of the Iraqi population. The Kurds are Sunnis but not Arabs. They comprise about 20% of the population and are hated by the former Sunni elites under Saddam as well as by ISIS today. Saddam gassed over 5,000 Kurds in the village of Khalabja. The Kurds will not forgive the Sunni Arabs for this.

The Shi'ites who today control Iraq since the overthrow of Saddam Hussein in 2003 are about 60% and hate the Sunnis who slaughtered them in the hundreds of thousands during Saddam's rule. In 1991, then-president George Herbert Walker Bush told the Shi'ites to rise up in revolt against Saddam Hussein and said that the US would stand by them. The US did not stand by the Shi'ites, and so over 100,000 Iraqi Shi'ites were slaughtered by Saddam in the south of Iraq. The Shi'ites will never forgive nor forget this American betrayal.

We see in the failed presidency of Maliki in Iraq, an expulsion, backed by the US of all the former officers in the Iraqi army under the Ba'ath and Saddam Hussein, leading to a new sectarian Shi'ite army, hated by the Sunnis and not trusted by the Kurds in the north.

97

The rise of ISIS or ISIL happened after the US tried to revive a Sunni military participation through something called the "Sunni Surge." After being trained and financed by the US, these graduates of the Sunni *Surge* rushed to join the Sunni ISIS, returning to the tradition of Sunni domination of Iraq and the renewal of killing of the Kurds and Shi'ites. We also see all the other so-called moderate Sunni groups joining ISIL as well.

This is an age-old tradition of 1,400 years in Islam for Sunnis and Shi'ites to kill each other.

At this point, I wanted to juxtapose the realities of the Islamic world with the politics of the United States, Canada, England and other Western democracies including Israel.

There is a saying that power corrupts, and absolute power corrupts absolutely. In America and the Western democracies, there is a tradition. Every few years there are elections. If the party in power loses popularity for whatever reason, it is voted out of office. There is no killing in the streets. It's almost like a baseball or football game.

In my opinion, all political parties are corrupt. But the corruption never has a chance to get too deeply rooted because the voters cut the corruption and vote for the rival party, which is also corrupt! Then the party that wins the elections has four or eight years to rule or misrule and then in turn gets voted out of office. We see the alternatives with the Democrats in office followed by the Republicans followed again by the Democrats, etc. The power is corrupt but never absolutely corrupt because the democratic system allows for periodically replacing political leaders when they become distasteful and unpopular.

But in the Middle East there is no democracy, other than in Israel. My wife, Rachel, has picked up broadcasts in which the Saudis say: *"Democracy in the Middle East...*

Never! Over our dead bodies because there is no democracy in Islam!" One of the fallacies of George W. Bush was that he thought he could bring democracy to Iraq after the defeat of Saddam Hussein. To bring democracy to Iraq, Islam has to first be removed. The same happened in Germany in 1945 after the fall of Nazism. Nazism is irreconcilable with democracy, but when Nazism was defeated, democracy was possible in West Germany.

But as long as Islam is in place, there can be no democracy. Democracy and Islam are irreconcilable, period. When the Sunnis are in power in Iraq, they kill the Shi'ites. When the US says that it wants democracy in Iraq, that means that the 60% population of Iraq which is Shi'ite must replace the Sunnis, and instead of being magnanimous in victory as Winston Churchill used to day, the new Shi'ite leadership of Iraq then goes on to kill the Sunnis who are only 20% of the population in retaliation for the Sunnis killing the Shi'ites for decades and centuries. The Kurds for their part use this perceived weakness by both the Sunnis and Shi'ites to develop their own regional autonomy and perhaps one day, independent state. The Kurds are a people of about 20 million and do not have an independent state yet.

According to Western thinking, the ideal situation for Iraq would be a system of proportional representation for the Shi'ites, Sunnis and Kurds, but that would require love, forgive, and forget, but I believe this is impossible for Iraq with 1,400 years of hatred and bloodletting. The only solution for Iraq and other Islamic countries is a system of loving, forgiving, and forgetting. It's called Judeo-Christianity. The Europeans succeeded in creating such a system after over a thousand years of killing and WWII. The US overcame the hatreds of the Civil War in 1861-65. "Get over it" and move ahead seems impossible in Islam.

99

There is a saying in the West: *"To every problem there is a solution."* In the Middle East the saying goes like this: *"To every solution, there is a problem."*

In Yemen, we see Iran backing the Houthis, another Shi'ite Islamic group struggling for its rights against the dominant Sunni regime in Yemen.

So Iran is sending its tentacles into Lebanon, Syria, Iraq and Yemen, in addition to its attempts to encircle the Sunni Saudi Arabia by infiltrating the Sunni Gulf states, such as Kuwait, Qatar, Dubai, Abu Dhabi etc.

Again these are the makings for a *perfect storm* in the Arabian Peninsula and the Fertile Crescent.

Before I conclude Chapter III, I wanted to address the so-called "Arab Spring."

Earlier in this book, in Chapter I, I spoke about the fallacies in American policy. And of course, if America is supposed to be Christian in its thinking, but then goes ahead and adopts mammon (oil and cash) as its god, then it will make grievous errors in policy.

I spoke about six million Jews being sacrificed in WWII for Arabian oil and support against the Nazis. Then there was the Cold War with the Soviets in which the US had to "sacrifice" Israel to do a balancing act with the Arabs to keep the Russians at bay. Then after the fall of Soviet Communism, we saw the "Pax Americana" in the Middle East in which virtually all the Arab countries became one with the US State Department, again at the expense of Israel.

We saw then-President George Herbert Walker Bush and then-Secretary of State, Jimmy Baker III, refusing to assist Israel in its humanitarian relief works of then-Prime Minister Yitzhak Shamir in providing housing for about one million refugees emigrating from Russia to Israel. James Baker III was quoted as saying: *"F**k the Jews. They don't vote for us anyway."*

In 1997 President Bill Clinton forced then-Prime Minister Benjamin Netanyahu to give up 80% of Hebron to the Palestinian Authority, something which caused Netanyahu to lose his political base and thus fall from power in the Knesset, leading to new elections in 1999 in which Ehud Barak came to power with the assistance of James Carville who was sent by Clinton in direct interference in Israel's political system.

After the year 2000, President George W. Bush was famous for his quote: *"Palestinian State in 2008"*. Neither he nor Secretary of State, Condoleeza Rice could be counted as friends of Israel, but were supporters of the Palestinian-Arab-Islamic agenda. All of this was before the election of President Mubarak Hussein Obama in 2008.

My wife, Rachel, also picked up Saudi broadcasts in 2006, in which they said: *"We will have a Moslem president in the White House in 2008."* My wife thought the Saudis were crazy! The world in general, and the American people in particular, didn't have a clue, and I believe today in 2015, still don't have a clue, except for religious Jews and Christians and political conservatives who can't put the pieces together regarding this Moslem president.

In 2010, a year after Obama's visit to Egypt, former Egyptian Foreign Minister, Abul Gheit, appeared together with Moslem Brotherhood representatives in a debate on Egyptian TV Channel 3.

The Moslem Brotherhood people were condemning Mubarak for 30 years of his rule and especially Mubarak's failure to terminate the peace agreement with Israel to wage war or Jihad against Israel.

Abul-Gheit answered them thus: *"You Moslem Brotherhood people are all like little children. You don't know how to rule Egypt. And if one day, Allah forbid, you do come to power, you will destroy Egypt. But let me calm you down. I had a one on one meeting with Obama last year (2009) and he swore to me that he is a Moslem. His Kenyan-born father was a Moslem* (Sunni). *His step-father Soetoro was a Sunni Moslem from Indonesia. Obama was raised in a mosque and a madrassa until age 11 in Indonesia.* (Remember the words of Francis Xavier who said: "Give me a child until 10 years of age, and I will make him a man." Obama was made a Moslem man by age 11 in Indonesia.)

"And Obama told me clearly: 'I have economic problems after the collapse of Wall Street in 2008, and Obamacare problems. But when I overcome these economic problems: I swear I will show the Moslem world what I am going to do to Israel!" (Destroy it).

Indeed in a very short time thereafter, Wall Street returned to 12,000 after having fallen to 6,000, I believe because of the agreement with the Saudis to "float" Wall Street with incredible amounts of cash.

Rachel also has been picking up Saudi broadcasts throughout the Obama years in the White House that he had three "orders" or commands from the Saudi King: 1. Replace the Iranian Shi'ite regime with one more malleable and user-friendly to the Saudis and the West, preferably under UN supervision; 2. Destroy Israel; 3. Islamicize America.

The ideal situation for Obama is to paint Israel into a corner regarding Iran so that Israel would have to attack Iran and then both countries would "duke it out" leading to both countries being destroyed by each other while the US, under Obama, would just wait it out and come out smelling like a rose. Kill two birds with one stone. Then all Obama would have to do is Islamicize America, with the Saudis basically ending up owning America.

Obama's appointment of Hillary Clinton as Secretary of

State from 2009 to 2013 left us with no positive memories. We have the famous joke of the "reset button" with the Russians, and of course, the tragic abandonment and deaths of four American diplomats and heroes in Benghazi, Libya in 2012 at the hands of fanatic Moslem terrorists. Supposedly they were killed by people who were unhappy with a movie produced about Islam.

But as far as I am concerned, Hillary Clinton was just continuing a multi-decades-old tradition within the US State Department of bashing Israel, regardless. Nothing Israel could do was good. Whether it was building communities in Judea and Samaria, building homes in Jerusalem, Israel was always wrong. Even Secretary of State John Kerry blames Israel today for all the evils of the Middle East.

Hillary Clinton's approach, like that of her predecessors, was that building across the Green line (the June 1967 borders) must stop. Settlement activity must cease. And all of this, in light of close to half a million Jews living already across the Green Line and natural growth. Building was taking place in areas where there was a consensus about the three major settlement blocs which would remain in Israel regardless of any negotiated agreement in Ariel, Maaleh Adumim and the Etzion Bloc.

One day in February 2011, a Tunisian fruit-vender was arrested for supposedly not having a license to sell in the street. What really was happening was that the arresting policeman wanted a bribe. The fruit-vender had his produce, cart, and scales confiscated. He was then slapped in the face by a Tunisian policewoman.

Having lost his honor by being slapped in the face by a woman, in addition to losing his livelihood, as soon as he was released he went to a gas station, bought a bottle of gasoline, poured it over himself and self-immolated.

Within minutes, You Tubes, Facebook, and Twitter accounts were appearing with pictures of the self-immolation. The whole country went up in flames. The Tunisian people had had enough of the 23-year rule of dictator Ben Ali, who immediately fled to Saudi Arabia.

This was the beginning of the Arab Spring. The next day, Libya went up in flames of revolution and soon after Egypt, Syria and Yemen.

Here we had a situation that could not be blamed on Israel! Everything was turned upside-down. Hillary Clinton and the State Department did not have a clue what to do about it.

Gaddafi was killed. Mubarak was imprisoned for a number of charges and only recently had his case overturned, and he was released. But Egyptians were fighting Egyptians in the streets of Egypt. (In Isaiah 19: verses 1 and 2 it says: "Egyptian will fight Egyptian. Brother will fight brother. Neighbor will fight neighbor. City will fight city." And this is a prophecy taking place to this day in these same countries in the Middle East.)

All of this was taking place while Hillary Clinton was in charge at the State Department.

In my opinion, God was "reshuffling the deck" just as the US State Department was tightening the rope around Israel's neck.

After the resignation of Hillary Clinton as Secretary of State, pressures began to build up again on Israel. And God reshuffled the deck again by bringing to the fore this new horrible organization called ISIS or ISIL, an implacable terrorist organization declaring itself as the Caliphate.

This organization is inherently an extension of Saudi Arabia and its Shariah Law. We see barbaric killings by fanatic Sunnis of Shi'ites, Christians, Kurds, Yazidis, and even fellow Sunnis. Just as the Shi'ites of Bashar al-Assad mercilessly kill fellow Syrian Sunnis, so, too, do the Sunnis mercilessly kill all others as well as themselves.

The United States really didn't know what to do about all this mess, so they brought in Iran to try helping to contain and shrink ISIS-ISIL with some success. But Iran remains a threat to the Sunni Saudis, to Israel, and the Christian West led by the US.

We see the US and the West backing the Sunnis vs. Russia and the Chinese backing the Shi'ites. The two main world power blocs are trying to use the insane Moslem blocs as proxies. And of course, the insane Moslem blocs use the Western nations and the Russians as proxies to fight each other in what, God-forbid, might become WWIII.

The Iranian Shi'ites consider themselves poor, pure, and Puritan. They consider the Sunni Saudis as infidels, heretics, and infidels for the following reasons.

Firstly, the Saudi Sunnis are the guardians of the holy cities of Mecca and Medina, something that infuriates the Shi'ites, who claim that the life style of the rich Saudi family is profligate, with princes flying all over the world for gambling, drinking, and prostitution, something they cannot get at home. As soon as their jet aircraft cross back over into Saudi airspace, they then don their royal galabiyas (gowns) and all their other appropriate Saudi dress and pretend again to be pious, whereas they are considered hypocrites by the Shi'ites who see the Saudis as corrupted by Western, immoral influences.

Secondly, the kingdom of Saudi Arabia has a foreign work force (or slave force if you will) of about 10% of the population. This working force is primarily from Hindu India (pagans) and Catholic Philippines (infidels) and the very presence of these non-believers is considered by the Shi'ite Moslems as a contamination and defilement of the "holy" Islamic land of Arabia. The Shi'ites say: *"Either expel this non-believing element or we Shi'ites will behead all of you, Sunni royal family members, as well as non-believing slaves."*

Thirdly, the Shi'ites say that the reason the royal Saudi family deserves to die is because they are collaborators with the Christian One World Government and economy. The Shi'ites claim that Islam is subservient to the Christian West (which also includes China, India and Japan which are not Christian) because Saudi Sunnis sell oil to the economies of the West thus perpetuating Christian hegemony over the world. Deny the West the oil, they claim, and Islam wins. So the bottom line is that all the royal Saudis must be killed by the Shi'ites who are coming to Mecca and Medina and replace the corrupt Sunnis with the "pristine" Shi'ite Islam.

I believe the royal family of Saudi Arabia should be concerned. This is a fight to the finish between the Sunnis led by the Saudis and the Shi'ites led by Iran.

In conclusion, we see Iran slowly but surely taking over more lands in Lebanon, Syria, Iraq, as well as in Yemen, in a sort of pincer movement around Mecca and Medina, the holy cities of Islam in Saudi Arabia. The Shi'ites are more to the north, east and south, while the Sunni Egyptian army is to the West ready to intervene to save the royal Saudi family. At the same time, Sunni ISIS is also to the north fighting against Shi'ite forces there and will also move southward into Arabia to save Sunni Islam in Arabia and confront Iran and the Shi'ites, but I believe that ISIS will also terminate the corrupt royal family and declare their caliphate, their version of Islam in the Saudi Peninsula.

All are about to converge on Saudi Arabia for *"High Noon,"* the final gun battle and showdown between Shi'ite Islam and Sunni Islam. Both sides lose.

CHAPTER IV

SAUDI NUCLEAR MISSILE BASE AT AL-SOLAYIL OASIS

I begin with an article by Ronen Bergman (translated by Avi Lipkin) from the Israeli Hebrew daily *"Yediot Ahronot"* of March 27, 2002:

"The Al-Solayil desert oasis has been turned into a military base. Over the last few years, launch pads have been added including access roads, command centers, a huge residential neighborhood. In addition a total territory of 1,400 square kilometers has been added, including unlimited bunkers for the storage of long-range missiles. The most recent peace initiative bestowed upon Saudi Arabia the image of moderation, but is only one side of a duplicitous game it is playing. Intelligence sources are disturbed, but official Israel, under heavy US pressure is keeping silent.

The computer at the command center of the CIA at Langley, Virginia, USA, chooses random code-names for subjects and operations it is following. "Deep Blue" is the codename for a cluster of worrisome pieces of information that have been received at the Agency since the beginning of 1988. The source of most of this information — comes from eavesdropping conducted by the National Security Agency (NSA) for monitoring signals of the administration and the military of China. According to these signals, Saudi Arabia has been conducting advanced negotiations with China for the purpose of purchasing dozens of ground-to-ground missiles capable of carrying nuclear payloads.

The intelligence communities of the US and Israel were thunderstruck primarily because until that stage, they knew nothing about this. At the CIA and at the technical level of the Israeli Military Intelligence research division, compasses were taken out and radii drawn. The missiles that the Saudis intended to purchase, CSS-2 as they are called in the professional language, Dong-Feng 3, have a range of 2,500-3,500 km. The whole Middle East, parts of the former USSR and of course, all of Israel are under the range of this missile.

The US and Israel did not understand why Saudi Arabia, professing a moderate political stance, needed this missile, that at that time represented China's vanguard atomic offensive weapons. The concern increased when these reports were reconfirmed by the generous financial support the Saudis were providing for the development of "the first Islamic bomb" as Pakistan's atomic program was described.

Israeli and US intelligence undertook broad, all encompassing operations with a double objective: Collecting details regarding the purchase and an attempt to learn what the Saudis really intended to do with the missiles. The operation was partially successful. It turns out that the Saudis purchased 120 missiles, and with them 12 launchers. A special surprise was in store for the US, when it became clear that the Saudi negotiator was none other than US State Department favorite Prince Bandar bin-Sultan, the charming ambassador in Washington.

The Saudis paid a fortune for the missiles. The Chinese received from their Saudi interlocutors the feeling that money would not be an obstacle and that Prince Bandar would pay any amount that would gain entry for his country into the prestigious (atomic-ballistic – VM) club.

THE BLOOMING OF THE DESERT WITH MISSILES

The first CSS-2 missiles arrived in June 1990, and were deployed in two places, south of Riyadh: Most at the giant complex built north of the Al-Solayil desert oasis, about 500 km from the capital, and a smaller quantity at Al-Jofar, 100km from the city. The remainder of the missiles arrived later.

About two weeks ago, "Ikonos" the best civilian photography satellite in the world, took a series of the photographs at the behest of "Yediot Ahronot" over Al-Solayil. The pictures were sent down from the heavens, and are shown in this article for the first time, proved that over the last few years the Saudis have invested tremendous amounts in developing the "King Khaled" secret military city.

Compared to previously available pictures of the region, taken by the French satellite "Spot" in 1995, the intensive construction in the region stretching over an area of hundreds of square kilometers in the desert is clearly visible. The Saudis added missile launchers, approach roads, command centers, a huge residential area, a mosque for engineers and members of the staff, as well as a new and tremendous area, full of incalculable bunkers with conventional and non-conventional weapons, with a storage capacity of over 60,000 cubic meters. East of Al-Solayil, out of the range of the cameras, is a Saudi Air Force base with two squadrons of Tornado jet fighters.

The enormous missile base has a support area and two launching areas 6 km apart from each other which are positioned in narrow and hidden ravines.

There are 33 buildings in the support area. Eight of them are buildings large enough to store the CSS-2 missiles that are each 24 meters in length. The launch area includes scattered buildings and a concrete launch pad.

In each of the two launch areas, a 50-meter-long unidentified building covered over with earth was located. So were two underground missile storage warehouses, as well as garages and two large support buildings.

In comparison to the photographs taken in 1995, a large expansion is noticeable in the administration and residential areas. It is possible to clearly see command installations, residential areas, a large mosque, soccer field, a specious park, car parking lots and more. The airstrip of the local airport has been lengthened to over 3km (2miles).

The weapons storage compound, spread out on over 1,400 square kilometers, is much too large to be merely a CSS02 missile base, and it evidently serves other secret purposes. It is possible to identify clearly more than 60 fortified buildings for weapons storage.

For a long time, it was not clear to American intelligence where the Saudis were hiding their missiles. At first it was thought they were at the Al-Harj Air Force Base complex, about 50 km south of Riyadh. Only ground level intelligence and pinpoint satellite surveillance led the CIA to the secret military city of Al-Solayil. The "Ikonos" pictures were received according to the coordinates that were obtained beforehand by American intelligence.

The updated information, already in the hands for some time of the Israeli and US intelligence services, was the cause for not inconsiderable headaches. This was reinforced after September 11th, when it became clear to everyone, really to everyone, that it could happen, and there are those who are sorry today about the obedient line Israel adopted regarding Saudi Arabia because of US pressure.

ALL ENEMIES AND OPPONENTS ARE BOUGHT OUT.

The purchase of the missiles was part of a general Saudi trend to achieve military power, which turned it at the beginning of the 90's into the biggest purchaser of weaponries in the Third World after Iraq.

The US Administration felt betrayed. For only a few years after the great efforts by President Reagan, to ratify the sale of AWACS early warning aircraft to the Saudis, all of a sudden this deal pops up, contrary to the declared policy of Riyadh, and on the surface with no practical purpose.

The furious Americans asked for clarifications. The Saudis explained that they needed the missiles in order to defend themselves from Iran (then thought of as the most serious regional threat), and that it was decided to purchase them from China, after the US refused to sell them F15 fighters in 1985. In the end, it is true that 24 planes were sold to them but the missile project, said the Saudis, was already underway.

King Fahd promised that Saudi Arabia would not place chemical or nuclear warheads on these missiles, nor would they use them in a first strike. In order to lessen concerns even more, Saudi Arabia signed the nuclear non-proliferation treaty. (NPT) The king promised not to take part in the development of atomic bombs, and also promised that after the missiles were in place, that military activities at the Al-Solayil area would cease.

Fahd, how should we say, did not exactly keep his word. The Saudis promised they would allow US inspectors at the Al-Solayil site, if Washington

110

would promise that Israel would not attack them, but in the end, they refused to allow inspections at the site.

After the Gulf War, the Saudis became the "underdogs" and succeeded in diverting the anger elsewhere, especially at Iran and Iraq. Neither did Israel in discussions with other countries raise the Saudi issue.

In 1990, when the missiles began arriving at Al-Solayil, Israel wanted to stir up a storm but the US was satisfied with assurances by King Fahd, and instructed Israel to maintain a low profile. Israel sufficed with a protest, but this was just a drop in the ocean compared to the campaigns it was waging against countries such as Syria and Iraq.

In the case of Saudi Arabia, details about its involvement in the Pakistani atomic project became known, and that Saudi Arabia was bankrolling terrorist organizations. It was also clear that the House of Saud was beyond any doubt corrupt to the foundations, and lusted for unrestrained power buying out any and all enemies and opponents. The US kept silent and forced Israel to the same.

For the Saudis, September 11th reshuffled the deck. Many in the US, in and out of the Administration felt free to get off their chests something that had been accumulating for a long time. Four months ago, it was Pentagon strategist Richard Perle who said: "in my opinion, the Saudis are not part of the solution. They are part of the problem...We had all reasons to assume that they were grateful for our saving them during Desert Storm — and we were wrong."

The Pentagon did not limit itself to declarations. Updated photos arriving from "Ikonos" point to massive building of American bases in the Gulf. For example, the giant airbase at Qatar was intended to replace at least partially, the bases in Saudi Arabia.

PUTTING THE EGGS IN ALL THE BASKETS

Publicity about what is happening in Saudi Arabia, together with the enormous anger following September 11th, caused a deterioration of the prestige of the Saudi regime, which was supposedly western and enlightened.

Leading analysts in the US press published highly critical columns about the royal house.

But the Saudis were quick to recover. Dr. Uzi Arad, formerly head of the research branch of the Mossad, and political adviser to Prime Minister Netanyahu, knows the subject from up close: "The Saudis operate a well-oiled lobbying and propaganda machine in Washington. They correctly identified the shortfall as a result of the terrorist attacks and were quick to counterattack.

"The publication by Thomas Friedman about Prince Abdullah's initiative must not be seen as merely incidental, but as part of a much wider sophisticated process which was intended to restore the status quo ante showing Saudi Arabia again to be a moderate and pragmatic country, and to turn it into a primary axis between the US and the Arab countries."

The new political initiative, with its virtual Middle Eastern innovation, does not, from the Saudi perspective, conflict with its continued support for terrorism, well oiled kowtowing, to regional powers, as extreme and crazy as they might be.

This is basically a duplicitous game, the only purpose of which is the continued hegemony of the Saud family in the Arabian Peninsula, by means of putting the eggs, and there are many of them, in all the possible baskets.

Professor Yossi Kostiner, Head of the School of History at Tel-Aviv University, has been dealing for years with the Saudi regime: "What we are dealing with here is very tough tribal/male-oriented politics. The Saudis are placing the emphasis on defending the regime, by means of diplomacy, shrewd politics and caution, and not necessarily by means of force.

In his words, "US forces in the Gulf as well as the emergency facilities, intended for receiving additional forces, are intended for protecting the kingdom from a military challenge, primarily from Iran or Iraq. Iraq attacked Saudi Arabia with missiles, and Iran took over control in 1992 of the Island of Abu Musa, at the entrance to the Persian Gulf, and it is administered since then by both countries.

In spite of the confidence in the strength of the US, and that it will not allow Saudi Arabia to be conquered, there is an attempt by the Saudis to flatter the Iranians, in order to keep the latter as a regional counterweight to the Iraqis."

(Avi Lipkin comments: This article by Ronen Bergman was written just before the US invasion of Iraq in 2003 and the termination of Saddam Hussein's rule. And it appeared in my third book written in 2003, *"Islamic Threat Updates Almanac #1 – 5763"* Today, Iraq, or at least the Shi'ite eastern part of Iraq is now merely an appendage of Iran. So Iraq, per se, is no longer an aggressive threat to Saudi Arabia.) The article continues:

"Beyond the danger of a frontal military confrontation, the Saudis identify other threats to the security of the Saud dynasty: a revolution from within, or terrorism supported by groups like Al-Qaeda or from states like Iraq.

"The Saudi desire to ensure quiet with the help of flattery or much money is directly opposed to US policy in the region. In spite of this, the Americans acquiesced to the relations with Iran, and also later swallowed the Saudi support for terrorism."

The duplicity of the Saud family expresses itself in nearly all fields. For external purposes, the Saudi administration puts on a display of enlightenment, western behavior, and its representatives are most active in European diplomatic communities and in the US. The Saudi oil barons often give orders in London and New York. But on the other side, there is a darker reality, and the relationship with Iran and Iraq is an excellent example of this.

At first, Saudi Arabia explained its purchase of Chinese missiles as a reaction to the Iranian aggression towards Saudi Arabia. When asked whether he would give orders to use the missiles, King Fahd responded: "If we are forced to, we will. Our patient opposition should not cause the Iranians to think that we are weak. We are hoping they won't make problems for us, because we don't want to test the will of our people to defend themselves."

On the other hand, Saudi Arabia has over the years adopted a position of compromise toward Teheran – and this position became stronger with the election of Khatami as president. The Saudis today support Iran financially, issue fraternal declarations with the Khomeinistic Islamic regime, and oppose any US initiative to attack it."

(Avi Lipkin comments: Remember this article was written in 2003. Things have changed radically since then.)

The same applies to Iraq. In spite of the hatred felt by the leadership in Riyadh toward Saddam Hussein, whom they see as a megalomaniac, who broke the basic rules of the tribe, and in spite of Saddam's attack on Saudi Arabia with missiles, and threatening to invade their territory, like he did in Kuwait, the Saudis today (2003) are doing everything they can to torpedo the expected American attack on Iraq."

(Avi Lipkin comments: In my opinion, and I deal with this in my first and third books, the American invasion of Iraq in 2003 was in response to the Saddam Hussein state terrorism attacks on the US: First attack on the World Trade Center in NY in February, 1993, the Murrah Federal Building in Oklahoma City on April 19th, 1995, the shooting down of TWA 800 in the summer of 1996, and more…)

MASSIVE SUPPORT FOR TERRORISM

For years, Saudi Arabia was not in the center of Israel's concerns. The US, on the other hand, knew well what was going on there, and according to assessments by Israeli sources well-acquainted with the CIA, it was clear that there was a system of commissions between the princes and themselves, as well as toward outside elements. The Americans saw clearly just how corrupt things were, and the ease with which it was possible for officials in the Riyadh regime to earmark giant budgets from this clause to another clause in order to cover themselves.

An investigation published about three months ago in the "New Yorker" revealed US National Security Agency eavesdropping tapes during the 90's. The broadcasts paint a picture of a regime that is growing increasingly corrupt, distancing itself from the people, from the religious. A weak and frightened regime, it is ensuring its future by paying off hundreds of millions of dollars in protection to extremist organizations seeking its overthrow.

In 1996, Saudi funds supported Osama bin Laden's Al-Qaeda, as well as extremist organizations in Afghanistan, Lebanon, Yemen, central Asia and throughout the Persian Gulf.

According to the "New Yorker", in 1994, Mohammed Al-Hilawi, first secretary of the Saudi delegation to the UN, defected and sought asylum in the US. According to his lawyer, Michael Wilds, he brought with him 14,000 internal government documents, showing royal family corruption and human rights violations and support for terrorism. He claimed that he was in possession of proof that the Saudis had provided technical and financial assistance to the Hamas, and a meeting was held in the office of his lawyer with two FBI agents and an assistant District Attorney. "They were given samples of the documents, and we put them on the table," Wilds said. "But the agents refused to receive them." The lawyer and his client did not hear from the federal agencies ever again. Al-Hilawi, who won asylum, now lives in hiding.

From a series of secret internal memorandums of the FBI, made available to "Yediot Ahronot", it turns out that in 1992 it was already then clear to American intelligence that Saudi Arabia was a supporter of Hamas. Thus, for example, in a memorandum written by the FBI special agent Robert White, of the Anti-Terrorism Task Force of the FBI in Chicago, that in 1993, Mohammed Saleh, one of the heads of the Hamas in the US, received $110,000 from a mysterious Saudi association by the name of Faisal Financial, registered in Geneva, Switzerland, to his account number 8060700 at the "National Bank of Chicago." Behind the association, according to the FBI, is a group of Saudi banks, with the full knowledge of the regime in Riyadh.

In another case, mentioned in the memorandum the Hamas asked to circumvent strict US laws against organized crime and money laundering. For that purpose, the members of the associations entered into complex and Gordian business deals in real estate, the only purpose of which being the transfer of funds into the US, without this being registered as such in the bank computers, and being exposed to the scrutiny of the FBI.

"The Koran Institute", identified by the FBI as a front organization of the Hamas, undertook a series of money transfers under the direction of a Saudi businessman, Yassin Kadi, the president and owners of "Kadi International" which serves actually as a front for the Saudi government. With the completion of the deal, $820,000 was transferred from Mr. Kadi, who created a labyrinth of front companies to the "Koran Institute," and from there to the Hamas.

Professor Kostiner: "There is no doubt that the Saudi administration knows exactly what the Hamas is. They pay ransom to many organizations, and according to the information in my possession, they actually had a working arrangement with Al-Qaeda. True, Bin Laden was expelled from Saudi Arabia, and his citizenship was revoked in 1994, but his family, which continued to maintain close relations with him, allowed him to continue to work, and in exchange, Al Qaeda did not act against Saudi Arabia.

(Avi Lipkin comments: According to the book *"Osama Ben Laden: The Man Who Declared War on the US"* by Yosef Bodansky, US President Bill Clinton cut the same deal with Osama Ben Laden by which the US in the mid-1990's paid off Ben Laden with megabuck taxpayer dollars for Al Qaeda to take its terrorism elsewhere. This also helps to explain the cover-up regarding the Islamic and Saddam Hussein connection to the first WTC truck-bombing in February 1993, the Oklahoma City bombing in 1995, and the shooting down of TWA 800 in the summer of 1996. Clinton wanted the US economy to prosper, and so he paid "protection" to Osama Ben Laden to ensure "industrial quiet". The Saudis did it, the Europeans did it. Clinton did it. The only problem is that the chickens came home to roost with the attacks on September 11, 2001 because President George W. Bush refused to pay up like Clinton did.)

"The Saudis have been doing this for a long time – all the way back to the 60's, in other words, since the money, the big money began to accumulate in their coffers. They buy out their enemies, they bribe and reconcile, and alongside this, they support Islamic causes. In the 1970's they succeeded in this way to aver PLO attacks against Saudi Arabia.

"To a certain extent, the Saudis got themselves into a trap. The moment they paid ransom once, they could not refuse the next time, and they created a list of individuals and organizations now on the payroll for industrial quiet."

And when Saudi involvement was required for the investigation of attacks, this help was not given happily. Examples are not lacking.

On April 7th, 1995, the Americans were sure that Imad Mughnieh, operations officer for the Hezbollah and no.2 most wanted in the world, was that close to being apprehended, tried and perhaps given the electric chair. That same day, he was flying with MEA (Middle East Airlines) from Khartoum, Sudan to Beirut, Lebanon with a scheduled stop in Riyadh. Sources in the FBI told us that the Saudis foiled the plan, and prevented the plane from landing in the kingdom claiming that there was a malfunction in the airport's technical computer.

An extreme lack of cooperation was also noted during the investigation of the attacks against the US Army base at Dhahran in 1996, where 19 American soldiers were killed, as well as a year before at the Khobar Towers, where 7 people died. FBI and CIA teams arriving to investigate the incidents reported a cold Saudi attitude, hiding evidence, and a feeling that from Riyadh's perspective, it was preferable to bury the whole affair quietly. The Americans solved the riddle of the attacks, carried out by the "Saudi Hezbollah". The royal family really did have that to hide.

The attack on the USS Cole in 2000 was perpetrated by Saudi citizens of Yemenite origin. Here, too, the Saudi security services did not assist in solving this case.

But the peak was after September 11th when the Saudis refused to assist in checking the backgrounds of 19 men, half of whom were Saudi nationals, who took part in the attacks on the World Trade Center and the Pentagon. This group is just a tiny part of the thousands of Saudis who have joined the extremist organizations throughout the world.

BRIBERY OPENS UP ALL THE PANTS
Beyond America's need for Arab support, there is another matter causing

it to be hesitant in any matter involving Saudi Arabia: Big Saudi money that has been "invested" in Washington, DC over the last 30 years. Fahd's regime was a big financial contributor to the aggressive campaign waged by the Reagan administration, headed by the CIA head William Casey, against what appeared to be a Russian presence in South America, and in the war of the US against the Soviets in Afghanistan.

Even when the oil revenues decreased considerably, the Saudis had enough money to be able to approach the right elements in the American capital. A senior American official said this week: "A Saudi diplomat once smilingly quoted to me an Arab saying: 'Bribery opens up all the pants.' It would be interesting to conduct a survey about the number of senior people in the administration during recent decades, who have not slipped into their pockets, or into organizations for whom they were seeking favors, Saudi money.

"This is not clear or blatant bribery. The Saudis can finance for this or that secretary a festive lecture at Harvard University and to pay him $50,000. If he is not able to receive these monies during his term of office, he is assured of a career as a lecturer when he retires. (Look at former president, Bill Clinton today.)

The Saudis and their friends in the oil industry play an extraordinary role in the Texan administrations of the Bushes. For example, the Texas company "Haliburton", has a number of subsidiaries active in Saudi Arabia. This company was run for many years by Vice President Dick Cheney.

During the Clinton Administration, the situation was similar. The Saudi government donated $24 million to Arkansas University, which was close to the president's heart. The Saudis also acquired Boeing aircraft in the billions of dollars, and assisted his administration in a number of initiatives of his in the Middle East.

According to Bob Barr, formerly a senior operations person in the CIA, the CIA was asked during that time not to conduct any dangerous intelligence gathering operations in Saudi Arabia, and in effect became almost completely blind to what was taking place among the royal family.

Bar was appointed in 1993 to CIA station director in Dushanbe, Tajikistan, on the border with Afghanistan. He related that we watched hopelessly the

Islamic fundamentalists who preceded the Taliban, who were supported by the Saudis, as they were building the training camps, mobilizing supporters and were conducting campaigns in countries bordering the former USSR. His reports and warnings were received with apathy.

The Saudis never scrimped anywhere in the world, and they displayed a special involvement in parts of Yugoslavia. They were the first to respond positively to requests by the leader of the Moslem majority in Bosnia, Alija Izetbegovitch, for financial aid and they assisted in undermining the embargo that prevented Bosnia from arming itself legally. The result: Today there are more religious Moslems in Bosnia than there were in 1992, and what used to be historic mosques, became again active worship mosques and not only museums for tourists. New, shining mosques are being built, usually in the kitsch style of the Persian Gulf. Thus, for example, the new Saudi mosque in Sarajevo, which looks like a space station, is so different from the local tradition. Also, Islamic educational centers have popped up one after another, in Sarajevo and other cities.

The number one organization for financing terrorist activities in Bosnia is the "Supreme Saudi Committee for Welfare." On October 18th, 2001, hundreds of peace force soldiers surrounded the Committee for Welfare offices in Sarajevo, shot the locked doors open and broke in. Large trucks brought to the site, were loaded up with the contents of the offices — computers, documents, lists, pictures, videotapes. Everything including $200,000 in cash that were hidden away in a safe were confiscated.

From a meticulous search of the documents, it was revealed that Saudi private and governmental sources had sent, through the Committee for Welfare, more than $800 million since the end of the civil war in Bosnia. There were clear lists as to what to do with the $600 million, and "according to the material that was confiscated, we fear very much that the rest of the money was used for terrorist purposes," said senior sources in the Bosnian government.

STOCKS IN THE "ISLAMIC BOMB"

As for the Pakistani atomic project, more is hidden than visible. The excellent relations between Pakistan and Saudi Arabia stretch out to many additional aspects of intimate military cooperation, including Pakistani military visits to Saudi Arabia, unilateral declarations of the regime in Riyadh in favor of Islamabad.

American and Israeli intelligence investigations regarding this affair began in the middle of the 80's, when it became clear where Pakistan, a poor country, was obtaining the enormous amount of funds needed for the project. From the Saudi perspective, this was a continuation of the traditional policy of supporting religious objectives ("The Islamic Bomb") involvement in important projects in the area and flattering an influential power that would soon become a nuclear club member.

On November 22nd, 1990, President George Bush Sr. received a highly classified document, which dealt with the possibility of arming Chinese missiles with Pakistani nuclear warheads on Saudi soil. The Saudis, according to the information, feared Saddam Hussein so much that they demanded from the Pakistanis that they deliver the Saudi share or "stock" in the atomic project.

To this day, it is not clear if this information was accurate or false. Everyone agrees that the scenario is not impossible. According to the information that has accumulated in the US, that the Saudis not only paid between half a billion to one billion dollars to the Pakistani atomic project, but they also made sure to "grease" the hands of one private person, the chief scientist Ahmed K. Khan, who is also connected with the Iranians.

A NON-CONVENTIONAL WARHEAD AIMED AT POPULATION CENTERS

The CSS-2 missile (Dong Feng 3) is the main weapon of the Chinese non-conventional arsenal. It is based primarily on the Russian missile R-12/SS-4 (In spite of the fact that the Russians refused to sell the missile to China, the latter attained the technical details necessary, evidently through espionage to produce the missile). The missile was test-fired for the first time by the Chinese at the Shuang Shi Tso site in 1967.

The missile is propelled by liquid fuel, which is relatively easy to store, in four engines with a propulsion force of 64 tons. The missile may be launched directly from within the storage facility (such as Al-Solayil) or from a mobile launch pad.

The missile was designed to carry a nuclear, chemical or biological warhead as well as conventional warhead, and was intended to provide an answer to a possible threat from the USSR. It is not an accurate missile, and has a range of error of 2.5 km. In light of this, the missile is not intended for pinpoint targets but rather large targets such as highly populated areas.

This missile is also used by the Chinese for launching satellites into space and there are at least two versions of this missile. The first has a range of 2,650 km and flies at an altitude of somewhere between 100 to 550 km and carries a single nuclear warhead weighing 2,150 kg.

In 1983, the Chinese initiated a program to lengthen the range of the CSS-2 to 3,500 km. The payload, according to some reports can include 3 nuclear warheads.

The last experimental launch took place on August 21st, 2001, when China conducted the largest-scale war games in the last decade. The Dong Feng 3 was fired from the test grounds in northern China, and US military satellites followed it until it landed near the Mongolian border.

When the sale of the missiles to the Saudis was leaked, the then deputy Foreign Minister Wu Shuwa Qien, adamantly defended the sale: "The Saudi government has promised us they will not transfer the missiles, will not use them in a first strike, and will only use them in self-defense. We believe Saudi Arabia will keep its word.

"The sale of the missiles", added the minister 'would contribute to stability in Saudi Arabia in particular, and the Middle East in general."

About a thousand Chinese engineers participated in building the site, and today as well, there are at the site on a permanent basis, Chinese engineers, responsible for the ongoing maintenance of the missiles. A thirty-year contract between the two nations was signed.

THE BEST SATELLITE IN THE WORLD
The Ikonos satellite, which provided "Yediot Ahronot" with the pictures for this report, is the best commercial photography satellite in the world. This is the first commercial satellite that collects photographs with a resolution of one meter (yard). In other words, one can identify objects on the ground the size of

which is one meter, on condition that they are distant from other objects, and have special visual characteristics. Individual human beings cannot be seen.

The "Ikonos" was built by Lockheed Martin, and is operated by the "Space Imaging" company. The pictures were analyzed by John Pike, CEO and owner of "Global Security,"and Tim Brown, senior researcher of the company."

CHAPTER V

THE FINAL BATTLE FOR MECCA AND MEDINA

THE PERFECT STORM

In the first four chapters I gave a hint, a very imperfect summary, of the fallacies of American policy, the Russian approach, the horrible relations between Sunnis and Shi'ites, and finally the unknown Saudi nuclear project. All this will now lead up to the final battle for Mecca and Medina.

In my sixth book, *"Return to Mecca,"* I tried my best to analyze the second book of the Torah, Exodus, in order to prove that the Exodus of the Children of Israel took place in Arabia. I tried to show the original centrality of Arabia to the formative period of the Jewish religion (Mt. Sinai, Mt. Horeb, the Ten Commandments, the giving of the Torah, the Phylacteries which are, I believe, replicas of the Ka'abah black stone of Mecca) which took place in Arabia over a period of 38 years, followed by a two year journey northward and eastward to the east of the Jordan River, followed by the crossing of the Jordan River and the conquest of the Promised Land.

What I did not do was deal with economic, military, and political aspects of how Israel will be returning to Mecca after the showdown between the Shi'ites and Sunnis. So this, my seventh book, will actually serve as a sequel to my sixth book *"Return to Mecca,"* from a worldlier dimension.

But first, I wanted to review again some elements from my sixth book in order to make the connection.

I will never forget when Israel changed its currency from Israeli Pounds (lira) to Shekels in 1979, it minted a 100 shekel coin which later became a smaller 10 agora coin (after shekels were changed to New Israel Shekels in 1985) featuring a menorah on a piece of broken pottery found in an ancient archeological dig.

Palestinian terrorist leader, Yasser Arafat, came out with a seemingly ludicrous statement that instead of the menorah being on a shard of broken pottery, that it was really a menorah superimposed on a map of the Middle East with Israeli borders including Saudi Arabia!

We Jews thought that Arafat was crazy. We never claimed Saudi Arabia! But Arafat had this notion that we did claim Saudi Arabia. Most everyone simply disregarded Arafat's remarks.

In 2010, Jim and Penny Caldwell provided me with a quote from one of Osama bin Laden's speeches in which he was criticizing the Saudi leadership for hypocrisy. And it was a long speech, but I will only give a short quote relevant to this book:

"Thus Israel—and behind it, America—killed all the children of the world. And who is to stop Israel from the murder of our sons tomorrow in Tabook or in Jauf or in the surrounding areas of Palestine? And what will the rulers do if Israel starts to expand its unfair, unjust and false settlements— which the leaders do declare as such—beyond its currently known boundaries, and says, 'Our borders extend to Medina.'"

Interestingly, it should be noted that Tabook is in NW Saudia Arabia, the home of a major Saudi Air Force base, only a couple of hundred kilometers from Eilat (Israel) while Jauf is in northern Yemen!

The Caldwell's, during their time in Saudi Arabia claimed and have proven archaeologically that the Israelites traversed all of the Arabian Peninsula during their 38 years of wandering in the desert from the tip of Yemen, mentioned in the Book of Exodus as well as in Oman and all the way north to Basra in Iraq, also mentioned in the Holy Bible.

So now, not only Arafat is claiming that the Israel claims Arabian territory, but so does Osama bin Laden, extending, he claims, Israel's claims in Yemen as well. It seems every Moslem knows this.

This quote from Osama bin Laden's speech is what finally made me conclude that maybe there is something in his words and in Arafat's words that lend credence to the thought that Israel does indeed have a claim to the Arabian borders.

Then many other things began to happen that convinced me to write my sixth book, *"Return to Mecca,"* a book based on biblical, Greek, Roman and other sources proving thousands of years of connection of the Israelites to Arabia. The book did not discuss the actual political, military and economic breakdown of the Arab world that would lead to Israel's return to Mecca, but merely a scriptural, academic approach to a possible scenario predicted in the Holy Bible.

It is not my purpose to repeat my sixth book, but I think it would be useful to consider certain questions raised, in *"Return to Mecca"* and answer them here.

Was Jethro, high priest of Midian, a distant cousin of Moses? Yes. Are *Midian* and *Medina* one and the same? Yes. Did Moses marry Zipporah, daughter of Jethro, thus also a cousin? (A biblical and Middle East tradition) Yes. Did Moses fight in Cush (Ethiopia or Sudan according to Josephus and Yalkut Shimoni)? Yes. Did Moses marry a Cushite woman who was not Zipporah? Yes. Many rabbis mistakenly claim that Zipporah and the Cushite woman were one and same. Did Moses say to Pharoah the first time: *"Let my people go so that they might go around in circles in the desert?"* (Hajj) The answer is yes. Did Moses say to Pharoah *"three days in the desert"?* (The Hajj is three days.) The answer is yes. Are the phylacteries a replica of the Qa'abah black stone in Mecca around which Moslem pilgrims circle seven times as part of the Hajj? The answer is yes. Are there proofs from biblical scripture that Israel was indeed in Arabia? The answer is yes. Is Mt. Sinai/Mt. Horeb in NW Saudi Arabia within view of the Red Sea? The answer is yes. Did God say to the Israelites in Deuteronomy 2: *"Enough being encompassed around this mountain? Turn north and proceed to the land that I promised your forefathers."* The answer is yes. (Conclusion? We were to the south in Arabia). Did God say in Deuteronomy 11 and later in Joshua 3 that our borders would extend from the Mediterranean to the Euphrates River and from Lebanon to the "Great Desert"? (Saudi Arabia) The answer is yes. Did the prophet Elijah flee to Beer Sheba to escape Jezebel's edict to kill him? Yes. Did the angel of God tell Elijah that he had an additional 40 days and 40 nights of hiking in the wilderness to reach Mt. Sinai/Mt. Horeb? That would put Elijah in NW Saudi Arabia of today.

I beg forgiveness from my Jewish readers, but, doesn't it say in the New Testament that Mt. Sinai is in Arabia (Galatians 4:25) and didn't the Apostle Paul go from Damascus to Arabia and stay in the same cave as Elijah? Jim and Penny Caldwell were also there and documented everything!

Again, I beg forgiveness from my Jewish readers, but my wife, Rachel, and I watch many different Saudi Arabian TV stations from our dish satellite, and we see numerous kadis and imams talking about how Moses, Aaron and Jethro were "here" at the Qa'abah in Mecca.

Well if our feet tread there, didn't God say in Deuteronomy 11 and Joshua 3 that "wherever our feet tread would be for an inheritance for the Children of Israel?" And there are foot-markings or sandal-markings all over the Arabian Peninsula. The Arabs and Moslems get it, but we Jews don't know and don't want to know.

Unfortunately, Jews, especially religious Jews, want nothing to do with "contaminated" Christian or Islamic texts and traditions so we Jews as a people remain one dimensional in our thinking and to this day, I think I am the only Jew in the world who points clearly to the role of Saudi Arabia in our Exodus 3,500 years ago and to the inevitability of our return under circumstances set up by God, Himself. We must be three-dimensional in our thinking as well as inter-disciplinary. But until now we are not.

Should the fourth book of the Bible, Numbers, or Bamidbar in Hebrew (In the desert) be renamed in English to *"In the Saudi Desert?"*

All of these questions are raised and answered in *"Return to Mecca."* But all of that is history. And since the writing of that book in 2012, we are witnessing a tragic, historic process taking place in North Africa and the Arab Middle East of complete chaos, turmoil, death and destruction, something that was not caused by Israel, but by the inherent insanity and criminal psychosis that is Islam. The purpose of this book will be to provide different scenarios that could lead to the Judeo-Christian takeover of Arabia and its subsequent termination of Islam, again not at the initiative of the Jews or Christians but because of the collapse of Islam and the termination of misrule and genocides taking place today at the hands of different Moslem factions, which will inevitably all turn on each other in Mecca.

As I complete the writing of this book in May 2015, the Western powers and Russia are attempting to negotiate a deal with the Ayatollah leadership of Iran that will at least temporarily restrain Iran from becoming a nuclear weapons state.

I wrote about this in my third book: *"Islamic Threat Updates Almanac #1 – 5763"* in 2003. Even at that time, the Israeli leadership was talking about a nuclear threat to Israel from Iran. In that same book, I translated and reprinted an article by Ronen Bergman from Israel's largest newspaper "Yediot Ahronot" about a "secret" Chinese-built missile base at the Al-Solayil Oasis in the heart of the Saudi desert stocked then in 2003 with at least 120 Dong Feng missiles provided by China with nuclear warheads provided by Pakistan. Abdul Kadr Khan, the father of the Pakistani nuclear project, was paying back the Saudis for funding the Pakistani nuclear project.

So Saudi Arabia is already a nuclear-missile equipped country, something too embarrassing for both Democratic and Republican parties to admit since this was something that started in the early 1980's and was never mentioned in the American media.

This attempt by the West and Russia to negotiate a "restraining order" for Iran will fail and will be the catalyst for a nuclear arms race in the Middle East. Countries like Egypt, Jordan and Syria will all want nuclear tipped missiles. This is a prescription for a global cataclysm.

It is known that Israel has been restrained numerous times by the world powers from attacking the Iranian nuclear project through various means, but a bad agreement with Iran could lead to an Israeli response. All options are on the table. Even President Obama has said this numerous times. Maybe President Obama wishes to paint Israel into a corner leaving Israel no choice but to attack Iran alone hoping that

Iran and Israel will destroy each other, and America comes out "smelling like roses," having not had America intervene in another foreign war.

Hezbollah was created in Lebanon by Iran, after the Israeli invasion of 1982 to expunge the south of Lebanon of Palestinian terrorists. But Israel has faced an additional campaign in 2006 with the invasion of southern Lebanon with the killing of Israeli soldiers Regev and Goldwasser, Israeli soldiers on patrol on the Lebanese border.

Iran put Hezbollah up to this as a proxy to divert Israeli attention away from an attack on the Iranian nuclear project. Hezbollah became and continues to play the role of "useful idiots" for Iran.

The same applies to two operations in Gaza after the withdrawal of all Israelis from Gaza in 2005 under Prime Minister Ehud Olmert. Hamas in Gaza also became "useful idiots" for Iran to divert Israel's attention away from Iran.

We are now facing new wars with both Hezbollah in Lebanon and Hamas in Gaza. Iran is throwing all the useful idiots at Israel as it can, to keep Israel from attacking the Iranian nuclear project. Iran is doing its utmost to arm Hezbollah and Hamas as well as funding these two terrorist entities.

Until now, these threats from Hezbollah and Hamas have not been existential threats, and Israel has remained relatively untouched by the so-called "Arab Spring" now wreaking havoc on Syria, Iraq and parts of Lebanon.

But we do indeed see Hezbollah expanding its presence from Lebanon into Syria, Iraq, and Yemen to face off against the Sunnis: ISIS, Jabhat al-Nusra, Al Qaeda, etc. All these different Shi'ite and Sunni forces could at any time turn on Israel and start a war. Up to now, God has used these different Shi'ite and Sunni groups to attack each other, leaving Israel relatively untouched.

In biblical times, we saw the armies of Ammon, Moab, and Seir march on Israel, encompass Jerusalem, and then instead of destroying Israel, these three armies destroyed each other (II Chronicles, Chapter 20). And so now, this scenario is repeating itself as Sunnis fight Sunnis and Sunnis fight Shi'ites.

As mentioned previously in this book, former Secretary of State, Hillary Rodham Clinton spent much of her four years in the State Department attacking and blaming Israel for "everything." Then on February 11, 2011, the so-called "Arab Spring" broke out, something Israel had nothing to do with, and the State Department had no inkling of what was happening, where it was coming from, and who was to blame.

I called it: "God reshuffling the deck." When John Kerry became Secretary of State, he also renewed pressure on Israel and, lo and behold, *"ISIS later becoming ISIL, later become IS"*... something Israel had nothing to do with in its creation and again the US under President Obama could do nothing to blame Israel.

As mentioned earlier, the US Administration under then-President George W. Bush, destroyed the Ba'athist regime of Saddam Hussein and expunged virtually all of Saddam's military officers from the military to hand over control to the Shi'ites who were previously slaughtered by Saddam's people.

As a result of this error, the US then tried something called the Sunni Surge to restore some kind of military autonomy to the Sunnis of Iraq, but this became ISIS-ISIL-IS. Any Sunni Arab who would not join this Islamic Caliphate would be beheaded as were Shi'ites, Christians, Kurds, and Yazidis. These Sunni terrorists became killers for the sake of killing.

On the Shi'ite side, it was Hezbollah, Bashar al-Assad and the Iranians slaughtering the Sunnis.

So we find a new reality today in the Middle East by

which the entire Arab Middle East is now imploding and its population is being decimated by these self-destructing rival Islamic groups: Shi'ite and Sunni.

At this time, half of Syria's population has become refugees and as of April, 2015, estimates stand at 230,000 dead Syrians from the civil war there that started in February 2011.

Since President Obama promised the American people that he would pull US troops out of the Middle East and Afghanistan, so the chaos and anarchy have become total. The US is hoping that Iran will come in and "clean up" the threat of Sunni ISIS, just as the US hoped that Sunni Saddam Hussein would defend the world from the Shi'ite Ayatollah Khomeini. And after all is said and done, the US and Western nations are returning their troops to Iraq and Afghanistan ostensibly for "training" the locals, who will all become ISIL in the end any way. The problem isn't the training. The problem is Islam which prevents any progress towards rebuilding these countries and helping the Moslems, themselves to rebuild their lives.

As a result of this chaos, we see millions of Arabs and Moslems fleeing the hell-holes known as Islamic countries and are fleeing to the Christian countries of the West in order to survive. *"The grass is greener on the other (Christian or Israeli) side."*

We see civil wars in Algeria, Tunisia, Libya, Egypt, Yemen, Lebanon, Syria, and Iraq with other Arab countries seeming to be volcanoes ready to explode.

Two countries which, it seems, remain unaffected are Jordan and Saudi Arabia. The Hashemite Kingdom of Jordan as well as Saudi Arabia are ruled by Arabian Desert Bedouin tribes and have highly professional Sunni armies.

However, up to 92% of the Saudi population openly favors ISIS/ISIL with a slightly less percentage in Jordan.

131

Again, the ideology of ISIS/ISIL is the ideology of Wahhabi Islam in Saudi Arabia.

As Iran closes in from the east in Iraq and the Kurds from the north of Iraq and Syria, I predict that ISIL is going to move southward and westward to take Jordan and Saudi Arabia. The popular support amongst the Sunnis is there for ISIS. The monarchies will be gone, because ISIS views these monarchies as corrupt and hypocritical.

As I mentioned previously in this book, if the goal of ISIL is to bring about an international caliphate and destroy Christianity, ISIL must then kill the world economy based on Saudi oil. This is where I believe the One World Government comes in.

Iran is now set up in Lebanon through the Hezbollah, in Syria through the regime of Assad, and in Iraq through the Shi'ite regime there, formerly through Maliki and now his successor Abadi, both Shi'ites. Iran is also sowing discord among the Shi'ites from Kuwait all the way down the Persian Gulf to Bahrain, Abu Dhabi, Dubai and Oman, where the Shi'ite populations are on par with the Sunnis and in the case of Bahrain, even greater in numbers than the Sunnis.

Now we see over the last year the rise to power in Yemen of the Shi'ite Houthis, also backed by Iran. So Iran is now in Yemen's capital, Sanaa, and moving northward, toward the Saudi border, eastward towards Aden and southward toward the Straits of Bab al Mandeb. Iran now controls the Bab al Mandeb Straits on the Red Sea, and are only an eight hour drive northward along the coast and then up into the desert to Mecca itself.

We are also receiving reports of the Egyptian (Sunni) Navy bombarding the Houthis (Shi'ites) in Yemen, as ships of the Iranian Navy approach the same area, something that could rapidly deteriorate into a naval armada battle between Shi'ite Iranian ships and Egyptian Sunni ships. The US navy is now sending in an aircraft carrier group as well.

So Saudi Arabia is being encircled by Shi'ite forces with only two Sunni forces able to confront the Shi'ites: Egypt and ISIS.

I believe we shall see a convergence of all these forces in a major battle to control the Arabian Peninsula with Mecca at its heart. This is a battle between Shi'ites and Sunnis for pre-eminence, until both sides self-destruct.

The Egyptian Army is ready to pour into Arabia just across "the pond". Saudi Arabia is paying Sunni Egypt dearly in cash for this alliance, cash which Egypt desperately needs. But when ISIS gets involved, I predict it will destroy the "corrupt" royal family of Saudi Arabia with its 6,000 princes turning one against the other and then destroying those who remain to make Arabia a purely pristine ISIS anarchic Caliphate.

Another important point about Egypt is that when the "Arab Spring" came to Syria in February 2011, the Sunni Egyptians said they would send in the Egyptian Army to intervene in Syria and overthrow Bashar al-Assad. So did the Turks.

But Iran threatened Turkey with an uprising of the Turkish Alawite/Shi'ites who compose 31% of Turkey (The Kurds are 25%) leaving Erdogan with a Turkish Sunni minority in Turkey of 44% having to contend with this uprising by the Shi'ite/Alawites and the Kurds, so the Turks backed away from invading Syria of Bashar al-Assad.

Similarly with the Egyptians, the Iranians threatened Egypt with a missile attack that would destroy the Aswan Dam thus destroying all of Egypt in the Nile Valley with a tsunami that would be released from the waters of Lake Nasser. This would give residents all along the Nile River a very short time in which to scamper a few miles eastward or westward to higher ground to avoid the massive floodwaters that would turn Egypt into desolation for 40 years as described in Ezekiel 29 sending 80 million

Egyptians into exile to the four corners of the Earth.

Iran in its megalomania is not afraid of Turkey, Egypt, Saudi Arabia, or even the US for that matter. Iran has said that even if half of its population was destroyed, *"Allah would still win."* We are talking about Iran being willing to sacrifice 35 million Iranians for its psychosis of world domination. But still, Iran's aim is to risk everything for Mecca and Arabia to become Shi'ite and thus displacing the Sunnis as preeminent in Islam.

But I believe the bottom line will be the destruction of the oil wells throughout the Arabian Peninsula by ISIS and the shutting down of the Straits of Hormuz by the Shi'ite Iranians that will drive gas and oil prices through the roof and threaten the very existence of the One World Government Economy. Ironically, this is something both the US and Russian oil producers want: to keep the price of oil high. The Europeans on the other hand disagree with this since the Europeans are net importers of oil except the UK and Norway.

At this point, I believe that the One World Government (OWG), in order to maintain steady oil prices and supplies, will "command" Israel to assist in the occupation of Arabia and to give a hand here by taking NW Arabia including Mt. Sinai, Mecca and Medina while they split up the Arabian Peninsula to be occupied by many world powers under the auspices of the United Nations in a manner similar to what happened to Germany after the defeat of Nazism in May 1945.

Again, my Jewish readers will forgive me for engaging in New Testament eschatology, but the "Harlot (OWG) slays the Dragon (Islam)." Otherwise the Dragon slays the Harlot, and it's the end of the world economy and the human race. Obviously, the OWG, for whom mammon is God, does not want the destruction of the world economy, because: *"It's all about money."*

This nonsense of Islam killing the Jews, Christians, Hindus, Buddhists, Blacks in Africa and then finally Moslems killing each other must stop. And Islam, I believe will be banned by the OWG as a threat to the world economy.

It will be at that time, I believe, that the OWG will say to Israel: *"Now you can build your Third Temple."* Islam will have been terminated and the OWG will say that the mosques on the Temple Mount on Mt. Moriah can be either dismantled or incorporated into the rebuilt Third Temple.

At this point I want to relate a testimony about how Moslems viewed Moshe Dayan after he handed the keys to the Temple Mount over to the Islamic Waqf.

After the Israeli victory in the Six Day War (June 5-10, 1967) the Moslem leadership handed over the keys (control) of the Temple Mount to the victorious Israeli Jews. The Moslems were sure, because of their untruthful propaganda that the Jews were going to slaughter them.

So the Moslem leadership handed over the keys. Within a few days, however, Moshe Dayan wished to show the Arabs that the Israelis were, as Winston Churchill said, *"magnanimous in victory."* This is a very Western behavior used with the defeat of Nazi Germany and Tojo Japan in 1945.

In the New Testament, there is the parable of *"Who is the king with 10,000 soldiers who goes to fight another king with 20,000 soldiers? Maybe it would be better to send an ambassage of peace?"*

Israel, outnumbered 100 to 1, had just won a miraculous war. But the numbers still remained 100 to 1, so Dayan thought it would be reasonable to extend the olive branch and make peace, while the iron was still hot. However, instead of them appreciating the *"magnanimous"* Dayan, the Arabs saw this as a sign of weakness. Rumors had it that the Moslems were beginning to reconsider their faith in Allah – Al Macker, or

Allah the greatest of all the liars and deceivers. After all, this time, the Arabs came to the realization that Allah had lied to the Arabs and Moslems and had given the victory to the Jews.

The God of Abraham, Isaac, and Jacob, the God of truth, was the one true God and not Allah the Liar or Satan.

But when Moshe Dayan used Western values and reason, the Moslems said: *"Aha! Allah has lied to and confused and deceived even Moshe Dayan, so Allah truly is the greater god (greater than the God of the Jews and Christians the God of Abraham, Isaac and Jacob,) and we shall remain loyal to Allah until the final victory."*

So the opportunity which temporarily existed, with the Arab defeat in the Six Day War, for leading the Moslems away from their liar god/Satan was lost.

My point here is that the war with Islam is not a war of the *flesh*, but a war of *spirit*. It is a war between God and Satan; a war between the God of Abraham, Isaac, and Jacob vs. the god Allah al Ilahi, or Allah the moon-god, war-god and sword-god or Mecca and Medina.

In my opinion, the way to end the war without bloodshed is to vaporize the black stone Qa'abah by killer satellite—laser— something that can be done without killing anyone.

Former US congressman Tom Tancredo spoke on 9/11 of "nuking" Mecca. I disagree with this. A killer satellite laser beam can do the trick of vaporizing the Ka'abah without killing even one person. I don't seek the deaths of the Moslems, but that they should be given a new life under Judeo-Christian Western Civilization and Democracy.

When the black stone is totally disintegrated, there is no more Islam because there is no more Hajj, or pilgrimage to Mecca, one of the Five Pillars of Islam. The head of the snake has been cut off. The God of Abraham, Isaac, and Jacob is greater than the god of Islam – Allah al Ilahi. And Satan-Allah has been sent to the pits of hell for a thousand years. Only then will there be peace on Earth. Again, my fellow Jews will forgive my borrowing of certain Christian terminologies taken from Judaism to prove my point.

The Moslem peoples of the world, like the Germans and Japanese of WWII will now be offered their freedom to be liberated by democracy and will now be blessed with a new life.Then the Third Temple can be built. I was once in a church in Springfield, MO, USA. A lady asked me when we Jews would rebuild the Temple on Mt. Moriah, and I answered, *"We can't just yet, the World won't allow us to."* The pastor sitting just behind me whispered, but just loudly enough for everyone to hear, *"Burn the mosques down!"* *"But Pastor,"* I explained, *"the world will not let us do it."* *"Burn it down now!"* he yelled out, to the hysterical applause of the congregants.

The Temple will be rebuilt in Jerusalem, when the Qa'abah has been disintegrated and Islam thus terminated. Israel will then be commanded, I believe, by the One World Government to build the Third Temple, since Islam will no longer exist, and therefore there will be no more opposition.

And Israel will liberate Mt. Sinai, the Mountain of God, as well as Mecca and Medina – NW Saudi Arabia.

Many Christians believe that the Temple must be rebuilt so that the "anti-Christ" will show up before the return of Jesus. So, many Christians support Israel in this endeavor of rebuilding the Temple in Jerusalem. Thus, time-wise this is a very exciting period for Jews and Christians to be alive. We are the generations witnessing more fulfillment of Bible Prophecy than any other generation in the last 2,000 years.

And yes, for the One World Government, it will indeed be a period of temporary great prosperity for the entire world at that time.

CHAPTER VI

RETURN OF THE JEWS AND THEIR CHRISTIAN SPOUSES AND CHILDREN TO ISRAEL

ISRAEL'S BIBLE BLOC PARTY IN THE ISRAELI KNESSET

I will never forget as a young Jewish boy in NY in the 1950's that we Jews in America were No. 2 after the Christians. It was that simple. There were 250 million Christians and 6 million Jews.

Until WWII, America was labeled as a Christian country but with the Nazi Holocaust and annihilation of six million European Jews, the US leadership decided on two corrective measures: Firstly, to recognize the Jewish State and secondly, to openly declare America to be a Judeo-Christian nation.

We mustn't forget that after the death of US President Franklin Delano Roosevelt in 1945, his successor Harry Truman could have bombed the railroad track going into the gas chambers, but still refused to do so, leading to the deaths of over one million maybe two million directly from that refusal.

Any disruption of the trainloads of Jews arriving at the gates of hell of those gas chambers and crematoria could have meant weeks of repairs, thus slowing the deaths of thousands of Jews every day. I am sure that that was on Truman's conscience when he decided against the advice of Secretary of State, George Marshall, on November 29, 1947 and voted in favor of the UN Partition Plan. In May, 1948, Truman decided to recognize the State of Israel. How could his conscience allow him otherwise after he was an accomplice to the refusal to bomb the railroad tracks to Auschwitz/Birkenau?

Secondly, in the US presidential elections of 1948, everyone expected Thomas Dewey to win. There were even headlines in the newspapers that Dewey won by 100,000 votes. But Truman won the elections because six million American Jews voted for him because he recognized the Jewish State! And this is where the myth of Jewish voting power took root.

So from 1948 to 1970, the Jews were indeed #2 in the US after the Christians, and everything seemed fine and dandy.

I moved to Israel in 1968. Two years later, I received information that the Moslems in America, in 1970, were now 100,000 in number. Not a problem… Jews were still six million.

Today, however, Jews are still numbered at six million, plus/minus, but the Moslems, I believe number 30 million!!! How did that happen?

Indeed, in President Mubarak Hussein Obama's inaugural address of January 2009, and you can check this out, he said that *"America today is a Christian-Muslim, Jewish-Hindu country."* America is no longer a Judeo-Christian country with biblical values. It is no longer *"One Nation under God"* but one nation under God *and* Allah. Isn't that wonderful? One nation under God and Satan! If you've read any of my books or this book leading up to this point, Islam, a Satanic system, has replaced the Jewish sister faith of Christianity.

Let's go back to the early days of American colonization. The Jews, many of them fleeing the Spanish Inquisition, came to New Amsterdam, now known as New York, or

Providence, RI, or Savannah, Georgia or Charleston, SC. We are recognizing almost half a millennium of Jewish participation in the colonization of the Americas.

In the American Revolutionary War, General George Washington came to the Jews of Philadelphia on Yom Kippur 1777 and told the Jews that the revolution was broke—bankrupt, and that if the Jews didn't go home to bring back all their gold, the revolution would be over and the Jews would be hanged together with revolutionaries by the repressive British troops. The Jews brought 30 million dollars of gold bullion and saved the revolution.

During Christmas 1777, 500 Jewish revolutionary soldiers stood bivouac while the Christians prayed in their Christmas services. So the Jews actively played a role in the revolution as well.

During the Civil War, the Jews disproportionately made up the officer corps of the Confederacy. When they asked Confederate President Jefferson Davis for permission to go home for the Jewish High Holy Days, Davis purportedly answered: *"God forbid! If you Jews go home, the Confederate Army collapses!"*

Also, during the Civil War, and in light of the above, President Abraham Lincoln established the Jewish chaplaincy in the Union Army. So the Jews actively played a role in the Civil War as well.

Jews have fought in all of America's wars. And today the Jews partake in all aspects of American life.

But the question remains, where are these Jews and their progeny of the last five hundred years? Most of them don't exist anymore, not as Jews in any event. They are now mostly Christians. Why: Assimilation. American Christians and Christian America have been so kind and loving to the Jews that the latter have simply intermarried

141

with their Christian compatriots and chosen to disappear.

So who are the Jews today in America? They are mostly from among the refugees who fled the persecutions of Russian Orthodox persecution and pogroms followed by Communism in Eastern Europe, those who fled from the Catholic Inquisition, persecutions, expulsions in central and southern Europe and of course the martyrs of the Nazi Holocaust.

Unlike the earlier Jews in America, the experience of the later Jews with Christianity and Christians was a horrible bloody experience. There was and, even today, there remains a gross ignorance by many Jews in America of the Protestant Reformation, and that new breed of Christians that loved the Jews, that knew Jesus was a Jew, and that the Bible was a Jewish book.

The phenomenon of Jews voting for Obama is a conundrum for America's Christians. But the Jews, who always voted for Civil Rights saw the election of a Black American as another link in a chain of minority candidates become president. Firstly, it was John Fitzgerald Kennedy, an Irish Catholic who broke the unwritten law of only Protestant presidents.

Obama has become the first Black American president. Most Jews in America today who are mostly Democrats would love to see a woman president in the White House. For many, it would be Hillary Clinton or Caroline Kennedy. Maybe one day there might be even a Jewish president. That is the Jewish thinking. Jews feel that the greatness of America is in its diversity, not in its traditions as a White Anglo-Saxon (WASP) nation.

But again, returning to America's Christians, Jews in America, most of whom are descendants not of the "old-timer American Jews," but of the more recent twentieth century immigrants from the Holocaust/European persecution Jews equate the Protestants of America who have always been kind to the Jews to those "awful" European Christians, mostly Catholic and Russian Orthodox who, persecuted the Jews in Europe.

So anything that reminds the Jews of America of any kind of Christianity is considered evil and off limits. "So Jews earn like Presbyterians, but vote like Puerto Ricans," like a minority and although Jews look like Whites and behave like Whites, and are looked at by the minorities as White,s they try to behave like minorities and oppose the silent Christian majority which in America is estimated to be about 70%.

So how do we get to a situation in the US and Canada of 80% intermarriage rates between Jews and Christians? In other words, for every 100 Jews getting married, 80 of them will marry Christians.

The answer is as follows: When Jews arrive in America or are born in America, they are offered all the possibilities to develop any career they wish.

The only problem is that they must work on Sabbaths and Jewish Holy Days, because America is not a Jewish country. In order to succeed in a new career, usually their Judaism must be second to their career, so they don't go to synagogue, they don't learn Hebrew, don't keep Kosher, and don't care about Israel.

Many people also study until they are 40 years old to be at the top of the class. Very often Jews are very focused on their studies and on succeeding in the "career." So many people marry late if they marry at all.

So if the Jews in America were six million in 1948, and over six million more Jews immigrated to America since 1948, and with natural reproduction, the Jews in America should be about 15 million today, but the truth is that the Jews remain at six million—in other words they have lost about 9,000,000 people as they fail to procreate as most other groups are doing. And very often, we are looking at mixed marriages where the children are raised as non-Jews.

The Jewish people are going through what I call a "Love-Holocaust" whereby we are being "loved to death" in America. No Jew has ever been slaughtered in the US for being Jewish. But what is happening is that to "succeed" in a career in the US, most Jews sacrifice whatever their Jewish background was in order to gain an academic degree or career. The cost: a peaceful Holocaust of Love of 9 million Jews in the US alone.

But even if the Jews reached a population of 15 million through natural reproduction and maintenance of the Jewish traditions, the Moslems today in the US would still outnumber us.

So let's look at how the Moslems have become 30 million. In 1970, the official statistics for Moslem population in the US stood at 100,000. In 1979, Jimmy Carter overthrows the Shah, and about 9 million Iranian Shi'ites, mostly secular people, people who "cooperated" with the American Christian enemy flee from Iran and most of which came to the US. So for argument's sake, let's say 9 million. The Sunni Arab Immigrants' Association claimed 7 million a few years ago. So that's 16 million – already outnumbering the Jews.

Louis Farrakhan and the Nation of Islam claim 4 million adherents – So now we are up to 20 million.

So President Obama is right: America is now a Christian-Moslem nation with Jews in third place and the Hindus in America very close to third place. The Chinese in America are also not that far behind.

But we haven't counted the Moslems in America who are not Iranian Shi'ites, Arab Sunnis or Black Moslems: such as Bosnians, Turks, Somalis, Chechens, Indonesians, Indians,

Africans as well as former Christian converts to Islam.

At this point, I must tell a few incidences of how Moslems enter the US.

My first example is perhaps the most important one of all. I was flying out of Dallas/Ft. Worth Airport and returning my rent-a-car on the second floor of the rental car port area.

A handsome and very friendly young man from Indonesia received the keys to the car, and as I was rushing to gather my baggage to catch my flight, he blurted out:

"America is the greatest country on Earth!"

"Yes," I answered. *"I already know that. Why do you say this?"* His response was: *"I used to deliver packages to the US Embassy in Jakarta, Indonesia. One day, an embassy official pointed his finger at me and said: 'Hey, you! Do you want to go to America? There is a flight leaving tomorrow. Bring your parents, your siblings, relatives. Let's fill up the flight. It's already paid for.'"*

The young Moslem answered: *"But I have no passport, no visa."* The official responded: *"It doesn't matter. We'll process you in America."* And indeed, this young Moslem Indonesian brought his entire family to America on that flight. Now, you tell me: *"Isn't America the greatest country on Earth?"*

On October 10, 2014, an article appeared confirming my story, but this time with immigrants from Somalia:

ILLEGAL MUSLIM IMMIGRANTS ARE BEING FLOWN INTO THE UNITED STATES IN EMPTY CARGO PLANES SAID A FIRED PILOT

"A pilot by the name of Dennis Welky was fired from his company by the name of "kalitta's" because he would not sign a waiver of his constitutional rights. They wanted him to fly in illegal Muslims flown into the United States in airplanes that have been marked "empty." According to Kalitta's own website:

"Kalitta Charters is an approved air carrier for the US Department of Defense, US Department of Justice and US Department of Energy, operating critical missions across the globe"

"When it comes to transporting critical cargo safely, securely and on time around the world, no one does it better than we do. After all, the Kalitta family began airfreight operations back in 1967. If it fits inside an airplane, we've probably flown it – and if we haven't, we've got the team to make it happen"

The following was posted by Tim Brown, published by "Freedom Outpost." The former Kalitta Charter pilot recalled Tennessee Rep. Rick Womick (R), a former Air Force pilot and commercial Boeing 777 airline pilot, admitted to flying five flights with Somali immigrants on board from London to New York City. According to Dennis, Womick said that flights would leave the US, land in the UK and be designated as empty for return, but the reality is that every seat would be filled with illegal Muslims. As he landed on the east coast as instructed, he would taxi right past immigrations and customs. The illegals were let off the airplane, given thousands of dollars, along with other benefits.

This is what is going on in our country today. Not only do we have 80,000 children crossing our southern border with a mixture of terrorists disguised as Hispanics we have this scheme to contend with. "Wow," It's continuously showing we have a bunch of hoodlums in the White House from Obama on down. Also from the same mentioned post and publisher: "We have also been aware that this lawless administration has paved the way for tens of thousands of Muslims from Syria to receive asylum via New Jersey."

My friends, this is bad, every time we turn around it's getting worse. This has to stop. This is what the major news networks should be investigating. Not following instructions from George Soros because he donates to them millions of dollars. We are losing our country because of these criminals in the White House because all they are interested in is creating a new voting bloc which could care less about conservative values. They have no values and they will always want us the People to provide for them because you will have the socialist politicians who will always cater to their vote. We must in a few weeks take our country back and start turning this Obama scheme to socialize America around."

The following is an interview on this same subject:

PILOTS FORCED TO TRANSPORT TENS OF 1000'S OF ILLEGAL MUSLIMS TO US — INTERESTING...

Published: Thursday, 23 January 2014 — State Rep. and Retired Commercial Pilot Both Acknowledge Pilots Being Forced to Transport Tens of Thousands of Illegal Muslims into the United States... (UPDATED)

"They taxied right past immigration and those people [the passengers] were literally led off and escorted off the airplane and they would give them thousands of dollars in their pockets."

This comes on the heals of the story that the U.S. State Department and the U.N. are working to resettle 30,000 "displaced" Syrians into the U.S.

Tennessee State Rep. Rick Womick and retired pilot, acknowledged his part in the forced transporting of illegal Muslims secretly to America. And he has devoted his political career to stopping this rape of this great country. "He was part of a team of experts coordinated by his D.C.-based Center for Security Policy that produced a report last year titled "Shariah: The Threat to America."

A U.S. pilot and employee of "Kalitta Charters" has gone on record of having lost his job for not agreeing to sign a TSA required consent form that would have him give up "a whole boat load of rights regarding security risk assessments as a United States American commercial pilot".

According to the pilot, whose first name is Dennis, at least one other pilot received the same information via company email and "went ahead and signed it" saying that he did not bother to read the consent form before he signed it because, "I need my job".

"Dennis" goes on to speak about being in a Baptist church listening to Tennessee Representative Rick Womick, who also still flies internationally as a pilot for Boeing, give detail accounts of returning trips from overseas with the "aircraft loaded, rock solid full, with every seat filled with illegal Muslims and flew it back to the East Coast of the United States".

If this is not explosive enough, Dennis continues to speak of Womick's account of what happened to passengers "after being instructed to land":

According to a 2011 WND article, Rick Womick "participated in a panel called "Defending Liberty in Legislatures," is an Boeing 777 airline pilot who has flown five flights with Somali immigrants on board from London to New York City." Womick has spoken out publicly that the U.S. Military should not allow Muslims.

It is interesting to note, that on Kalitta Charters website, they have these promotional statements: "Kalitta Charters is an approved air carrier for the US Department of Defense, US Department of Justice and US Department of Energy, operating critical missions across the globe"

"When it comes to transporting critical cargo safely, securely and on time around the world, no one does it better than us. After all, the Kalitta family began airfreight operations back in 1967. If it fits inside an airplane, we've probably flown it – and if we haven't, we've got the team to make it happen"

http://www.redflagnews.com/headlines/warning-shocking-empty-flights-filled-wmuslims-pilots-stripped-of-rights-forced-to-transport-tens-of-1000s-of-illegal-muslims-to-us-video?utm_source=twitterfeed&utm_medium=facebook#s thash.T8LdlHFF.2WNsKQNR.dpbs
http://www.wnd.com/2011/11/367193/

In another example, three lady friends of mine Joplin, Missouri told me about a rest area at mile-marker 4 on I-44, where the truck stops are and that two buses would arrive everyday in Joplin carrying Moslem immigrants bussed into the US from Mexico and transported up to the northern tier states.

The gatekeepers are bribed by the oil/Islamic agenda and the floodgates have been wide-open for decades. It's all about the trillions of dollars needed by the American economy to survive. The Islamic invasion of America is already paid for by the oil companies and Islamic agenda. The leaders who rule America are not Christians but serve mammon. Islam has the mammon. Therefore the leaders serve Islam.

Another example of Islamic infiltration is through the tunnels underground or land routes above ground from Mexico and Canada. Only God knows how many Moslems have crossed into the US with the help of "coyotes."

Last summer, after speaking in Abbottsford, BC, Canada just an hour's drive east of Vancouver, my hosts were driving me along the US-Canada border. They showed me the houses on the American side of the border clearly within sight.

I told my hosts about tunnels from Mexico into the southern US and my Canadian friends said that the terrorists buy houses on both sides of the US and Canadian borders, then dig tunnels between them and again, only God knows how many terrorists have crossed over into the US to carry out terrorist attacks when given the orders from Islamic Jihad.

A lady friend of mine in Maine told me about this shallow river demarcating the border between Maine and Canada and just how easy it is to wade across.

Once I spoke at United Baptist Church in Laredo, Texas. After speaking to services in English and Spanish, I was told at dinner about an interesting case.

One Sunday morning, early before services, church people arrived to find a woman wet from the waist down prostrate on the church carpet in the sanctuary. She was praying.

So the elders of the church spoke to her in Spanish thinking that because she had olive-colored skin she was from Mexico, but she spoke Farsi, the language of Iran.

Her story was as follows: She was born a Moslem into a well-to-do family and came to the Lord. When her family knew that she had converted to Christianity, they told her that she had to be killed.

Since she had a passport and was not married, she purchased an airline ticket to Paris, France. There, she purchased another airline ticket to Mexico City. Upon landing, she hired the services of a taxi driver "coyote" (immigrant smuggler) to drive her from Mexico City Airport to the American border at Laredo.

After the 16-hour drive, she arrived at the Rio Grande River at about 2AM. Her coyote driver took her to the embankment and told her to slide down the embankment, wade across the waist-high river, then climb the embankment and she was "home free" in America.

And that's what she did. She walked about half a mile to the United Baptist Church which is just off of Interstate 35 which begins in Laredo. She found the door of the church open and immediately went in to pray and thank the Lord for her delivery from death. The church leaders told her that she had to surrender to the authorities but that the church would vouch for her to receive asylum. Happy end to the story!

How many other people have been able simply to wade across the Rio Grande at 2:00 AM in the morning and not encounter any police or Border Patrol to stop her?

Finally, with the so-called Arab Spring, the US under President Obama is doing everything that it can to bring millions of Moslem/Arab refugees into the country with asylum, welfare, and a quick route to US citizenship.

One of the aspects of Stealth Jihad is that the Moslems don't boast about it. The Christians are asleep and the Jews are comatose to this phenomenon thinking that the Jews are still #2 and America is still a Judeo-Christian country.

At this point, I want to relate what I consider to be the second most important testimony in my life after the Dallas Council testimony.

I was driving my van in California during the summer of 1999. My route took me north on I-5 into Oregon, Washington State and then over the border into British Columbia with lectures virtually every night.

My plan was to speak one night only in Maple Ridge. From there I would drive up to Kamloops and Kelowna arriving in Edmonton, Alberta on Thursday, just in time to speak at a Baptist church. Finally I would spend Shabbat in a Jewish Orthodox synagogue in Edmonton.

Upon arrival in Maple Ridge, my hostess spoke on the phone with Kamloops and Kelowna and found out that the Jews in Kelowna opposed my speaking. Since this was to be a joint meeting of Jews and Christians in Kelowna, the meeting was then cancelled because of the "Liberal" Jews who opposed my message.

So I spent three nights speaking in Maple Ridge with what was to become my ten-hour presentation. Wednesday-Thursday I drove non-stop 20 hours to arrive just in the nick of time at the Baptist church there. It was a pleasant surprise that 20 Jews in Edmonton came to hear my message.

Friday morning, my local hostess, Cora Brisebois called the Orthodox rabbi to see if he could host me for the Sabbath. He answered in the affirmative, and I went over to his home.

His first question was: *"What is a nice Jewish boy like you doing in the Christian churches?"*

My answer was as follows: *"We Israelis are all war-heroes, but five million Jews in Israel vs. 1 1/2 billion Moslems cannot possibly succeed. But if we had 100 million evangelicals and born-again Christians on our side maybe that would level the playing field."*

The rabbi's answer was: *"God bless you, son! Good that you go to the Christian churches to mobilize support for Israel. I, personally, would never step in a Christian church, but if you do it, God bless you!"*

You see, it is forbidden for Jews to enter Christian churches according to the Talmud, but this is indeed a misinterpretation. What it says in the Talmud is that it is forbidden to enter pagan houses of worship. This was written around the year 500 AD/CE when all churches had statues in them … pagan houses of worship. But after the Protestant

Reformation five hundred years ago, the statues and icons have been removed. Since the Christians believe in the same God as we do: The God of Abraham, Isaac, and Jacob, and since they believe in the Tanakh or Old Testament, and since they believe in a Messiah who is a Jew, speaks Hebrew, and lives in Israel, that to me is no longer pagan!

Saturday morning, the rabbi announced my presence saying: *"We have with us today an Israeli Army spokesman, Avi Lipkin. The Christians give him ten hours to speak. Today at Kiddush after the service we shall give Avi ten MINUTES to speak!"*

When the time came to speak, two "Liberals" began to shout me down and would not let me speak! You see, Liberals with a capital L are liberal with you if you are liberal like they are, but if you are not liberal like they are, they are not going to be very liberal with you!!!

So I didn't speak.

Who came to the rescue? A Christian woman attending the Jewish Orthodox synagogue every Sabbath because Jesus went to synagogue on the Sabbath and not to a church on Sunday! Jesus read from the Torah, from the Haftorah and gave a sermon shortly thereafter. Nothing has changed in 2,000 years.

So, with my permission, she got up to address the group and said: *"If you are not going to let Avi speak, maybe you'll let me speak."* And they agreed. Her testimony was as follows:

"I am a social worker for the government of Canada, province of Alberta, city of Edmonton. I am a case-worker for a Moslem-woman-doctor from Cairo, Egypt."

"This female doctor was the Islamic equivalent of Mother Teresa. She would feed the poor and heal the sick. But unlike the Catholic nun, for whom the church was her

home and family and financial backing, this Moslem women worked in one of the poorest neighborhoods as a volunteer out of her own pocket. No one was supporting her. The poor people would bring her bread, cheese, eggs, etc, clean her house, do her laundry, but there was no financial backing."

"Being single and in her 40's, this doctor decided to emigrate to Canada to make a decent income after twenty years of volunteer work, just enough to qualify for a pension/ retirement at age 65, or so."

"After the emigration visa was approved by the Canadian government, there was a knock on her door. It was three 'Jihadis' or 'holy men' from the mosque where she prayed. She knew them, and they knew her."

"They greeted her saying, 'Mabruk' or congratulations. The doctor answered 'Allahi barak feek,' which means 'You, too, should have congratulations.'"

"Why do I have congratulations," she asked?

"Because we know you are going to Canada," they answered and continued saying, *"And we also have congratulations in store for us because you are going to work for us." "What does that mean?"*

They told her: *"You will have a clinic, the most popular clinic in Edmonton, Canada. Your fame will precede you. Jews, Christians and Moslems will all come to your clinic. You will know everyone in Edmonton. Your job will be to 'catalogue' the Jews and those Christians who are close to the Jews or love Israel. You will collect all their vital data for us on a disc and then give us the disc. When the time comes for Jihad, we shall kill all of them. The Moslems of Edmonton will be responsible for killing the Jews and Christians in Edmonton. The Moslems in Vancouver will be responsible for killing the Jews and Christians in Vancouver. The Moslems in Toronto will be responsible for killing the*

Jews and Christians in Toronto. The same applies for the rest of Canada, the US and any Jewish community anywhere in the world outside of Israel."

The doctor answered them: *"You guys know me. I pray every day at the mosque and give Zaqat (charity) as a good Moslem should. But I am not interested in politics, don't understand politics and am not interested in killing anyone... even the Jews. I am a doctor who swore the Hippocratic Oath to heal people and save lives."*

"So you're not going to work for us?" they asked. She answered in the negative.

So the three Jihadis with their turbans, long beards and Koran books in hand, grabbed another woman in her forties helping the doctor in the clinic, pulled out a knife, and slit her throat.

As the woman lay on the ground dead, with blood gushing out of her neck, the three Jihadis said to the doctor. *"If you don't work with us, this is what is going to happen to you!"*

The next day, Praise God, this doctor received asylum in the Canadian Embassy in Cairo, Egypt. The Royal Canadian Air Force flew in a private jet to pick her up and brought her to Edmonton to a safe house with 24/7 protection.

"And I am this Moslem woman's case-worker," said this Christian woman at this Orthodox Jewish synagogue.

She went to say that she works with the RCMP (Royal Canadian Mounted Police) and that according to their assessment, 90% of the Moslems in Canada are peace-keeping, law-abiding citizens. *"Only 10% of them are terrorists."* And these terrorists get their funding from the Middle East. When orders for Jihad are received, probably in coordination with 9/11 type attacks and a war in the Middle East, they will spring into action to kill all the Jews and those Christians considered worthy of death.

This was in the summer of 1999. This story was in all the news papers in Alberta, Canada but never made it into the newspapers in British Columbia or Saskatchewan, and of course, neither did it make into the US media. And yet this testimony is the second most important testimony of my life.

So let's do the math. If there are 30 million Moslems in the US and "only" 10% of them are terrorists that means that there are 3 million terrorists in the US. And if there are six million Jews in the US, how many of the six million Jews could be, God-forbid, massacred by the 3 million who are probably well armed while the Jews usually are unarmed?

We must remember that it took only 19 terrorists on 9/11 to paralyze the US. Islam has promised that the next attacks will make 9/11 pale in comparison.

And because the majority of the Jews in the US (78% voted for Obama), don't want to hear me because they are "Liberals" (stupid in my book), they do not have a clue of what is about to happen to them.

But in my opinion, whoever survives this Second Holocaust, will himself be moving to Israel or hiding in the hills somewhere.

If the killing of the Jews and the Christians close to the Jews takes place as part of a 9/11-like attack or series of attacks, it is my opinion that the law enforcement in the US, Canada, Latin America, and Europe will not be able, with the best of intentions, to protect the Jews and their Christian compatriots.

Since the Jews in the US are intermarried with the Christians at the rate of 80%, the Islamic terrorists will have no problem killing Christian spouses and children as well.

This is why I am predicting the shutting down of all the Jewish Diasporas outside of Israel when this all takes place. There are, in my estimation, about 7 million Jews living outside of the US with perhaps 3 or 4 million Christian spouses and children who also all face death and the hands of the ISIL type terrorists.

If they move to Israel, these survivors could feasibly add up to ten million Judeo-Christians to the already existing population of 6 1/2 million Jews and Christians already in the Land of Israel.

Therefore it is clear to me that a Judeo-Christian political party in the Israeli political system is inevitable. This will be a party that will represent the biggest constituency in the Israel political system when all is said and done. Just as the Diasporas in many countries throughout the world have shut down, so too will the turn of the Western Diasporas come soon.

God says in Hosea 11:10:

"My children, Ephraim, will come home trembling from the WEST as the Lord roars like a lion!"

God will use the Moslems as a giant spatula to scrape up the Jews and their Christian spouses and children from the Diasporas worldwide, and will bring them home to Israel from the four corners of the Earth.

When I was 15 years old, I had the opportunity to correspond with Israel's first Prime Minister David Ben-Gurion. My teacher at Hebrew school was Zvi Abu from the town of Tzfat (Safed) in the Galilee. He played a major role in turning me into a Zionist and helped me to write to Ben Gurion.

Ben Gurion's two letters changed my life, and at age 15, I already made up my mind that my future, as well as that of all Jews in the world, was in the Land of Israel.

Following are the translations

of the two letters.

The first letter is dated: January 8, 1964

Kibbutz Sde Boker

To Dennis Lipkin – Greetings

From your letter, I understand that you know Hebrew, therefore I will write in Hebrew.

It is true that it is possible for a Jew who lives abroad (outside of Israel) to be an honest, decent and scholarly person just as it is possible that a Jew who lives in Israel can be a bad unrighteous and ignorant person. However, if a Jew wants to really be a complete Jew, it is only possible in the Land of Israel.

In the U.S., the Jew is mostly a "Sabbath Jew", as opposed to a "Sabbath gentile", in other words, a part-time Jew living in a limited-narrow way. Only in Israel he is a Jew all the time and in everything he chooses to do.

In America, the Jew lives a life that is 99% American and this is the same with a British or French Jew.

Only here (in Israel) he is 100% Jewish because everything here is Jewish: the field is plowed and sown by Jews, the buildings are constructed by Jews, the roads are paved by Jews, the trees are planted by Jews, the books are printed by Jews and the baby from its infancy hears the Hebrew language and is exposed to Judaism.

Everything is immersed with Judaism, the physical and the spiritual, and there is no spirit without the physical and no physical without the spirit.

In America the physical and the spiritual that Jews are involved in or enjoy are 99% not Jewish.

A Jew who wants to be Jewish in everything – must come here (to Israel).

With blessing, David Ben Gurion

The second letter is dated: April 20, 1964.

(Kibbutz) Sde Boker

To Victor (Avigdor) Mordecai Lipkin, Greetings

I'm not a prophet and must not be a fortune teller, but I fear that Jews in the Diaspora will assimilate as time goes by if they won't have relatives in Israel.

I fear that Israel will cease to exist if the number of Jews will not double or triple. I do not have pictures here, but I will ask my friend in Tel-Aviv to send you my picture.

Respectfully, D. Ben Gurion

Indeed, David Ben Gurion *was* a prophet. In 1964, Israel's population was 3 1/2 million Jews and Christians. Today, we are approximately at 6 1/2 million Jews and Christians. So the population has doubled since 1964.

I predict that we shall double or triple again with the great wave of immigration yet to come after the Islamic Jihad begins the massive terror attacks in the West and then the Jews and Christians must flee for their lives to Israel.

I also believe that our borders will grow accordingly as the Islamic/Arab countries self-destruct and implode as we see already before our very eyes.

The Deuteronomy 11 borders will expand: *"From the Great Sea (Mediterranean) to the Euphrates, from Lebanon to the Desert (Saudi Arabia)."*

There will be room for everyone. I believe there will be great upheavals worldwide, but in the end, Islam will be defeated and banned. There will only be peace on Earth when Islam is defeated and banned. The Moslems are great people, but they need to get a life. We Jews and Christians will give

158

them that life they so much need, as they embrace the one true and only God: The God of Abraham, Isaac, and Jacob.

The Bible Bloc – Gush Hatanakhi Party at that time will be the biggest party in the Israeli political system, and the new Israel with the Deuteronomy borders will be a lush fertile crescent as it was thousands of years ago tended by God's children, the roots and the branches, the Jews and the Christians together. Israel's population will grow from more than six and a half million Jews and Christians to more than double or triple that, when all is said and done. Israel's borders will also grow to include the lands promised by God to the Children of Israel in Deuteronomy 11.

And somewhere along the line, the Messiah will show up for all Jews, Christians and human beings who wish to receive him on the Mount of Olives in Jerusalem.